Nature Calls Outside My Window,
A Collection of Poems and Stories

Nature Calls Outside My Window, A Collection of Poems and Stories

by

Suzanne Cottrell

© 2022 Suzanne Cottrell. All rights reserved.
This material may not be reproduced in any form, published,
reprinted, recorded, performed, broadcast,
rewritten or redistributed without
the explicit permission of Suzanne Cottrell.
All such actions are strictly prohibited by law.

Cover design by Shay Culligan
Cover image by Magnus Ostberg

ISBN: 978-1-63980-219-7

Kelsay Books
502 South 1040 East, A-119
American Fork, Utah 84003
Kelsaybooks.com

For all our family pets who gave us unconditional love

Also by Suzanne Cottrell

Scarred Resilience

Gifts of the Seasons, Spring and Summer

Gifts of the Seasons, Autumn and Winter

Acknowledgments

Thanks to my family for their encouragement and support. Special thanks to my loving husband Bob and daughter Sara for their ideas, photographs, proofing, and editing.

My appreciation goes to the Creative Voices and Taste Life Twice Writers' Groups for critiquing my poems and stories and inspiring me to keep writing.

I am grateful to Karen Kelsay and her team for publishing my first three poetry chapbooks.

My thanks to the following journals, anthologies, and their editors.

America's Emerging Poets 2018: Maryland, Virginia, and the Carolinas (Z Publishing House): "Commanding Vistas"
Botany of Gaia (Quillkeepers Press): "Murmuration," "Precision Pilots," "Solitary Walk," "Up a Tree," "Woodland Discoveries"
Exploring (Personal Story Publishing Project, Daniel Boone Footsteps): "Thundering Hooves in the Land of Giants"
Gifts of the Seasons, Autumn and Winter (Kelsay Books): "Beacon," "Nature Calls," Untitled: "Nightly woods' silence," "Scampering chipmunk," "Wintry Treats"
Gifts of the Seasons, Spring and Summer (Kelsay Books): "Precision Pilots," "River Gifts," "Secluded Berries," "Solitary Walk," "Symphonic Arrival," Untitled: "Chirping spring peepers," "Sultry summer's night"
Haiku Journal: Untitled: "Chirping spring peepers"
Harvest (Quillkeepers Press): "Garden Guardians," "Hungry Forest Percussionist," "Trapped"
Howl of the Wild (Winterwolf Press): "Longing for Your Call"
Luck and Opportunity (Personal Story Publishing Project, Daniel Boone Footsteps): "Breathless Moments"
Mingled Voices #6 (Proverse Hong Kong): "As the Shield Lifted"

NatureWriting: "Vigilant Hunter," "Where's the Pizza Party?" Untitled: "Great horned owl wakens"
New Plains Review: "Amber Eyes"
Nothing Divine Dies, A Poetry Anthology (Vita Brevis Press): "Backyard Morse Code"
Parks & Point: "Unexpected Visitors"
Plum Tree Tavern: "Nightly Eye Shine," "Wintry Treats"
Poetry Leaves: "Pearls in Flight," "Precision Pilots"
Poetry in Plain Sight: "Precision Pilots"
Poetry Quarterly: "Beacon," "Minuscule Moments," "Moonlit Marsh," "Remembrance," "Rescued Dog and a Poet," "Snake Pit"
Quail Bell Magazine: "Tenacity"
Remington Review: "Solitary Hunters"
Sapling (Quillkeepers Press): "Mother's Day Dilemma"
Snowdrifts (Quillkeepers Press): "Lake Dancers," "Temporary Traces"
The Avocet: "Beacon," "Woodland Discoveries"
The Pangolin Review: "Marine Illusionist"
The Remembered Arts Journal: "Captured Moment," "Indispensable Weed"
The Scarlet Leaf Review: "Secluded Berries"
The Weekly Avocet: "Leisurely Observers," "Nature Calls," "Pearls in Flight," "Pollinators' Delight," "Precision Pilots," "River Gifts," "Solitary Walk," "Symphonic Arrival," Untitled: "Chirping spring peepers," "Great horned owl wakens," "Nightly woods' silence," "Scampering chipmunk," "Spring peepers emerge," "Sultry summer's night"
Three Line Poetry: "Grazing in Yellowstone" Untitled: "Pristine snowfall blankets the land"
Trouble (Personal Story Publishing Project, Daniel Boone Footsteps): "Let It Go"
Twist in Time Literary Magazine: "Roaming Yellowstone"
What Is All This Sweet Work? A Poetry Anthology (Vita Brevis Press): "My Guardian"

Contents

Nature Calls	15
Pearls in Flight	16
Lake Dancers	17
Moonlit Marsh	18
Captured Moment	19
Breathless Moments	20
Marine Illusionist	24
Leisurely Observers	25
Lake Reflections	26
Skink Tale I	28
Skink Tale II	29
Skink Tale III	30
Solitary Walk	31
Woodland Discoveries	32
Snake Pit	33
Let It Go	34
Unwanted Passenger	38
Tenacity	40
A Garden Visitor's Grievance	43
Not You Again!	45
Precision Pilots	46
Symphonic Arrival	47
Pollinators' Delight	48
As the Shield Lifted	49
Remembrance	50
Indispensable Weed	51
Soaring Scavengers	52
Misunderstood Fowl	53
Backyard Morse Code	58
Where's the Pizza Party?	59
Hungry Forest Percussionist	60
Solitary Hunters	61
Secluded Berries	63

Trapped	64
Vigilant Hunter	70
Amber Eyes	71
Nocturnal Prowess	74
Escapee	76
Beaver Moon	82
Mitzi	83
Beacon	85
Rescued Dog and a Poet	86
Minuscule Moments	88
Mother's Day Dilemma	89
My Guardian	93
Up a Tree	95
Mutual Observers	99
Garden Guardians	100
Avian Immersion	101
Short Poems	102
Egrets	105
Thoroughbred	106
Nightly Eye Shine	107
Longing for Your Call	108
Unexpected Visitors	109
Commanding Vistas	113
Roaming Yellowstone	114
Temporary Traces	119
Wintry Treats	120
Once Millions Roamed	121
Thundering Hooves in the Land of Giants	122
River Gifts	125
Outside My Window	127

Nature Calls

Chilled air on an October afternoon.
Draped in a wool, Tartan shawl,
Sitting in my oak rocking chair,
On our rustic, wide, front porch,
Gently rocking to my own cadence,
Attuned to nature's varying rhythms.

Recognizing the familiar call
Of a flaming, red cardinal
Seeming to say, "Pretty, pretty, pretty."
The sporadic chattering of gray squirrels
As they protect their gathered seeds.

In the background is the constant buzzing, "REE . . ."
Of the male cicadas serenading.
The females are content to listen, like me.
Then the emphatic utterance,
The bass bellow of a bull frog.
Countered by the treble chirps of crickets.

A flock of migrating Canada geese
In their V-formation overhead
Honking throughout their synchronized flight.
The interrupting, hoarse caw of crows
Ravaging the corn field remnants
In my view across the gravel road.

Detached from the city's cacophony,
Calm and relaxed, I listen to nature's calls.
As a crisp breeze whistles through the trees
And tired leaves flutter to the ground,
My brief respite from household chores is waning.

Pearls in Flight

One morning country walk
sun rays pierced chilled, winter air
my breath suspended in puffs
formed miniature, translucent clouds
pale blue sky wore a string of
lustrous, freshwater pearls
while bellies of ring-billed gulls
streamed above bare treetops
within seconds the birds left
me beneath an unadorned sky

Lake Dancers

Reminiscent of an artist's comma brush strokes,
feathers of migrating Tundra swans fill the canvas of
the winter sky along the Atlantic Flyway.

Birds wear ivory suits, black webbed feet,
tap shoes, dance on the surface of shallow waters
before bodies slip among the waterfowl mosaic
on North Carolina's Lake Mattamuskeet.

Unlike Tchaikovsky's symphonic *Swan Lake,*
high-pitched honks deafen, whistles resonate
throughout the national wildlife refuge
as flocks forage for aquatic weeds.

Monogamous couples glide across
the shimmering ballroom floor,
mirror each other's movements.

Twilight approaches, the sun illuminates
swans to golden saffron, coral, tea rose
as lamps float and sleep upon the coastal lake,
their protected home until time for

their late winter departure
to arctic nesting grounds.

Moonlit Marsh

Moonlight trickled through
oaks, elms, and sweetgums
dressed in bright mossy skirts of
malachite-colored sequins.

Yellow and orange-red tubular flowers
of cross vine adorned their trunks.
Tree limbs swayed to sustained winds,
clattered with crescendo gusts.

Wind accompanied by
hoots of a barred owl,
croaks of bull frogs,
yips and howls of coyotes.

Raccoons, skunks, and
opossums promenaded
across the dance floor,
dense carpet of Asiatic dayflowers.

Southern lady ferns fanned
light green, lacy fronds.
Lemony fragrance of crushed spice brush
muted the earthiness of the marsh.

Sweetgum balls littered the ground
like party confetti.
When the moon bid good night,
calmness consumed the marsh.

Captured Moment

Had I blinked or looked away,
I would have missed
    the protruding arched back
    as a humpback whale breached
    frigid Alaskan waters.

Instead, I would have heard
    the onlookers clap and shout.
I would have heard
    the tumultuous crash of its
    forked fluke smack the surface.
I would have seen
    the splash and ripples.
I would have felt
    the wooden boat rock.

Instead, I spotted an extraordinary feat,
    a humpback whale propelled
    like a launched rocket.
My eyes widened, I searched Sitka Sound,
    hoping to glimpse another breach.

One exhilarating moment
in my mundane life
that took my breath away.

Breathless Moments

Eager to see whales in Alaskan waters, my family and I awoke early and inhaled our breakfast. We didn't want to miss the opportunity to watch the powerful, graceful leaps of humpback whales in Sitka Sound. We hoped Captain Ned would fulfill the brochure's promise of whale, otter, and seabird sightings. I smiled while hiding my apprehension of encountering migrating, forty-foot plus whales as we cruised in a thirty-five-foot boat.

"I hope we see some puffins, Mom!" said Sara, our thirteen-year-old daughter, wearing her puffin tee shirt.

My husband, daughter, and I boarded a boat at Crescent Harbor Marina on Baranof Island. Captain Ned and Molly, a naturalist, welcomed us and twenty-five other passengers. We chose seats near the front. After receiving life jacket instructions and the route itinerary, an elderly couple turned and asked, "Where are you from?"

Sara jumped up, "North Carolina. I've already seen a moose!"

"Sara, sit down," my husband said.

She huffed and sat down.

While the boat headed toward Kruzof Island, Molly directed our attention to a raft of sea otters floating within a kelp forest. Sara bounded to the window. Brown, fuzzy heads bobbed in the chilly water. We laughed and caught our breaths as a sea otter tumbled over on her back and rubbed her face with her front paws. Another one anchored in the kelp held a rock and hammered what looked like a crab resting on his stomach. We applauded the otters' acrobatics.

As the boat approached a rocky outcrop, I said, "Hey, Sara, aren't those puffins on that ledge?" I pointed to the black and white feathered birds with bright orange beaks and matching webbed feet, resembling circus clowns.

Sara giggled and bounced on her seat. "They're so funny looking they're cute."

"Sailors have called them 'sea clowns' and 'sea parrots,'" Molly said. "If you look closely, you may see some brownish-black chicks."

Sara waved her arms. "They look like little pom-poms."

I grinned, breathing deeply.

The roar of the twin-engine motor slowed to a low hum. As Captain Ned maneuvered the boat closer, we heard snorts and growls like a downtown bar brawl. Tan Steller sea lions jostled for positions on the sun-warmed rocks. Sara nudged, "They sound angry."

"I bet that bull weighs a thousand pounds," said my husband.

We watched as the hefty sea lion raised his head, grunted, and scared several pups into the water.

Captain Ned announced, "We're heading into open water now. It's going to get bumpy."

Trying to keep down my breakfast of smoked salmon quiche, I focused on Molly narrating the history of the Alaskan fishing industry. My knuckles turned white from clutching to stay in my seat.

"Keep a keen lookout for whales," said Molly.

As we scanned the sapphire water, my eyes and mouth opened wide. I gasped. Molly saw my face and shouted, "Whale breach!"

Sara tugged on my sleeve, "Where Mom, where?"

I had watched the arched back of a humpback whale as she propelled herself out of the water like a launched rocket, and then she smacked her forked fluke as she dove. My heart raced. My tongue wouldn't form words as I pointed to where only bubbles and ripples remained. *How can a creature weighing over a ton lift her body out of the water like that?*

"She's a mile away by now," Molly said. "Keep looking; they travel in pods."

"Molly, how did you know I saw a whale breach?"

"Only a grizzly bear or a humpback whale causes that expression."

"Excuse me, but can we go up to the observation deck?" asked my husband.

"Sure, but you'll want your jackets. It'll be windy."

We held onto the rail as we climbed up the steps single file. The wind carried the scents of salt and fish as it tried to push us back. We tucked our chins and pressed forward. My husband snatched his baseball cap as the breeze lifted the brim.

"Dad, can I have the binoculars?"

"Wait a minute," he groaned. "Look over there." My husband pointed as he planted his feet in a wide stance.

"Dad, let me see," Sara rose on her tiptoes. He handed her the binoculars and slipped the strap around her neck. The waves swelled.

My husband's brow furrowed. "Wait for it."

"Mom, did you see that?"

I pointed my camera northwest, held my breath, and steadied the camera as I captured a barnacle-tipped black tail in the lens.

"Whoa!" Sara said as the boat rocked.

We staggered to keep our balance. Then we heard a whale's explosive exhale and saw mist shoot up twenty feet as cormorants and a bald eagle soared overhead. I gasped, having lost count of the moments that took my breath away that July afternoon on Sitka Sound.

Marine Illusionist

Hidden in the shallows and tidal pools of the Pacific
Shy, scarlet, solitary creature with remarkable skills
Willed instantaneous color, texture transformations
Chameleon-like disguises among rocks, crevices
Clever impersonator, flexible escape artist
Graceful, fluid motion; sudden jet propulsion
Disappearing within a murky, inky cloud
Eight tentacles covered with suction cups, unyielding grip
Short-lived master of the sea, species preservationist
Intelligent Giant Pacific Octopus

Leisurely Observers

We lean against the top rail of a wooden bridge
that spans a pond rimmed with chartreuse reeds
and brown fuzzy cattails that sway in the breeze.
A musty, earthen smell pervades.

Motionless, dark olive shells, the size of Frisbees,
rest on a half-submerged log covered with moss and algae.
Eastern painted turtles with outstretched hind legs and webbed feet
like our Labrador retriever that sprawls in front of the air
conditioner.

The turtles relish the sun's warmth on this summer day.
Ah, to bask in sunlight without the fear of sunburn
or to drift in warm, shallow waters serenaded
by an Eastern Towhee, his familiar call of "Drink your tea."

We turn to the opposite rail and scan the pond's surface.
A beaked nose, dark shell, and spiked tail glide toward us.
The snapping turtle cuts through the murky water, creates ripples.
Atop the bridge, distanced from the water, we relax and watch,

Relieved our exposed toes are safe
from being misconstrued for tasty worms.
The turtle disappears into the shadows beneath the bridge.
We hasten to the other side and wait.

Despite the heat and the pond's invitation,
we choose not to enter the water,
content as mere observers
on this leisurely afternoon.

Lake Reflections

While we hiked the two-and-a-half-mile trail around scenic
    Price Lake
On a brisk October afternoon we spotted the emerald head
    of a Mallard drake

Stepped over a protruding hickory shagbark root
Glimpsed a scurrying chipmunk with his harvested loot

Paused to peer over a weathered bridge's wooden rails
At brown trout minnows pooled in the shallows and snails

The trickling mountain water of Cold Prong Stream
Beavers challenged its flow with their dam upstream

Paused to examine chiseled markings on a yellow birch stump
A steeper trail grade slowed our pace, required our arms to pump

Strolled along the boardwalk laid over marshy terrain
Sunlight streamed through evergreens suffering from acid rain

Recognized the need to become a partner for a remedy
To save the beauty of the lake and woods in jeopardy

Rounded the far end of the placid, mountain lake
A mound of boulders, remnants of a shifting plate

Listened to the gentle, lapping waves along the stony shoreline
A grey heron at water's edge sought a fish on which to dine

Scaled up granite slabs to our favorite vantage rock
We perched a safe distance from the edge while we took stock

Of nature's wonders, the grandeur of Grandfather Mountain set
    the stage
Canada geese honked overhead while we admired the beautiful
    mirror image

Of a collage of autumn foliage, mountain tops, billowing clouds
Reflected in the lake's clear, glassy surface far from urban crowds

A fish bit at the surface; concentric circles rippled
White pines sheltered us as rain drizzled

We followed the rolling, uneven wooded path
Hastened steps to avoid the rainstorm's wrath

As the trail wound its way through thick rhododendron and fern
An obstacle course of vegetation forced us to duck and turn

Reached the walkway across the dam by the Blue Ridge Parkway
The rain gradually subsided; a brilliant rainbow brightened this day

We looped through the campground; our hike neared its end
A memorable experience with stories to share, a trail
    to recommend

Skink Tale I

I peer onto our side porch,
where a skink basks
in the sunlight.

Thank you for devouring
mosquitoes, making my evening
porch sitting more pleasurable.

His streamlined body
with cream racing stripes
and his metallic, purplish-blue tail,

Signify his youthful age as he
scurries and slips into a crevice.
"Come back, I won't hurt you."

The timid skink remains hidden.
As my aging eyesight diminishes,
the skink's stripes will elude me.

His bright colors will fade
to subtle bronze like the statue
of an Olympic athlete.

Skink Tale II

A textured ramp to accommodate
our slow-paced, arthritic dog
serves as a reptilian racetrack.

Two common five-lined skinks
increase their speed as they
race to the finish line and disappear
into the lush, green foliage
of our orange daylilies.

What's your hurry?
To catch a cricket for lunch?
To play a game of tag?
To escape a hungry bird?

I shrug my shoulders.

Skink Tale III

With sleek, smooth, shiny scales
and a nub of a tail,
a common five-lined skink
clings with its clawed toes
to the wood siding on our house.

What happened to its tail?
A close encounter with a king
snake or a hungry robin?
How clever of her to detach
her tail, leaving it to wiggle,

A distraction to her predator,
while the skink escapes and climbs
to safety, like a starfish,
confident she'll grow a new tail.

Solitary Walk

After the trees clothe themselves
in emerald foliage, their branches
extend an invitation.

Tree oils and damp earthiness infuse.
Forest air offers reprieve from pollution.
Tree-lined path provides tranquility.

Wonderment of the woods embraces my being,
releasing me from worldly demands.
I discover apricot-colored hairy beards lichen
adheres to hickory shagbark,
spongy, yellow-green reindeer moss

cushions the forest floor.
Umbrella toadstools huddle.
Blue periwinkle florets decorate the ground,
aromatic sassafras awakens,
fuchsia rosebud delights,

puffy Carolina cherry laurel blossoms
appear cloud-like, buttery-yellow daffodils,
forsythias elicit sunshine, purple goblet
tulip magnolia blooms catch raindrops.
Eastern box turtle crawls from underbrush.

Five-lined skink basks in filtered sunlight on a rotting log.
Marbled salamander scurries to capture an earthworm.
My contemplative immersion, my renewal like the
revival of resurrection fern fronds.

Woodland Discoveries

Musty, loamy smell saturates the woods.
Damp leaves, moss cushion my steps.
Sunlight streams through partially bare branches.
Water droplets, fluid prisms, dangle
from remaining leaf tips. Plop upon my head.
I run my fingertips over tree bark scratches,
scars left by a porcupine.

Water gurgles in a creek,
overflows its banks from recent rains.
I take deliberate steps across
smooth, slick stones, logs
felled by industrious beavers.
I suspect a dam lies upstream.

I turn over a rotting log, hop back
as a spotted salamander scurries
under decomposing leaves,
wood frog clucks displeasure
at being disturbed.
I roll the log back into the mud.

Serrated holly fern leaves border my trail.
I spot burnished cambium where
whitetail bucks rubbed off antler velvet.
Giant, yellow hyssop curtsy in the breeze.
Squish, dark purple chokeberries
scattered by birds stain my boot soles.

I continue my hike over rolling terrain.
Striking blue asters cluster at base of a hickory tree.
Tiger swallowtail butterfly
flits from blossom to blossom.
I pause, drink some water, reflect on
my discoveries, woods' serene beauty.

Snake Pit

Water snakes reside upstream,
Rarely venture down to Snake Pit,
A good ole fashioned swimmin' hole,
Where the Watauga River runs wild and deep,
North of Boone off NC Highway 321.

Maneuver down the steep clay embankment,
Wedge one's feet between granite rocks.
A single knotted rope provides minimal assistance
To reach the mountain river's muddy shore.

The water hole accommodates many—
Hellbender salamanders, crawfish, trout, bass.
Water administers cold shock therapy
As swimmers plunge into the chilled pool,
Scream, flail arms. Most appreciate a
Refreshing dip on a hot summer day.

With numb limbs and bluish-purple lips,
Swimmers crawl onto huge, flat rocks
Bask in the sun and dry off.
Resemble turtles sunning on logs,
An enjoyable day at Snake Pit.

Let It Go

My husband had Memorial Day off, but I had to teach, making up for a snow day. I drank a whole bottle of water on my drive home, so as soon as I entered our house, I set down my bag and dashed to the bathroom. From the toilet, my peripheral vision caught a dark blob. I leaned toward the tub and saw what looked like a piece of black hose. *Why is a hose in the bathtub?* My pulse quickened after considering the possibilities.

I yelled to my husband who was grilling cheeseburgers on the front porch, "Bob, did you put a rubber snake in the bathtub? Not funny."

"If there's a snake in the bathtub, it's real."

My pupils widened; I gasped and hiked up my pants as I sprinted to my husband. "How did a snake get there?"

"What did it look like?"

"Black and slick."

"Sounds like a black rat snake slithered through a crack."

I cringed as I imagined a rat crawling through too. I tugged my husband's shirt. "You need to come look, now!"

"I'm starving, and the burgers are ready. I'll handle it after dinner."

"But what if he gets out? We might not find him."

"He's in the bathtub. He's not going anywhere."

My stomach churned. "You'd better be right. I don't want to see him slithering across the kitchen floor while I'm eating."

I bit into my cheeseburger and glanced at the floor. Even though I saw nothing, I pulled my legs under me and kept scanning the floor. *What if I had decided to take a shower?* I shuddered. "How can we remove him?"

"I'm not sure."

As soon as we finished eating, we headed to the bathroom. He examined the snake as the snake struggled to maneuver the smooth, sloped porcelain. Unable to get traction, he slid to the bottom. We noted the identifying white throat and chin.

With raised eyebrows, I stared at my husband. "You're not going to pick him up, are you?"

"No. He's not poisonous, but he can bite." The 4-foot snake vibrated his tail and flicked his tongue. "Get a garbage bag and the broom. I'll see if I can sweep him into the bag."

I grabbed my husband's arm. "Wait. You're not expecting me to hold the bag."

"Just get the broom and bag."

After I scurried to retrieve the items, my husband grabbed the broom. "Hold the bag open. When I get the snake inside, clamp the bag shut. Don't worry."

Rubbing the back of my neck, *I can do this.* I wanted to close my eyes, but I didn't dare. My husband nudged the snake. As the broom bristles brushed against the snake, he raised his head, opened his mouth, hissed, and struck at the bag. I screamed, dropped the plastic bag, and jumped back.

"Are you okay?"

"No, that snake almost bit my hand." I gripped the door frame with sweaty palms. My heart raced. "Just give me a minute." My husband swept up the bag and handed it to me. I asked, "Why don't you hold the bag, and I'll sweep the snake into it?"

He shook the bag at me. "Just hold it."

I squinted, leaned over the tub, and held the bag. My hands trembled. "Hurry, hurry!"

With one stroke, my husband swept the snake into the bag, dropped the broom, and snatched the closed bag from me. He twisted it and carried the bag away from his body as he left the house and walked toward the woods.

"What will you do with him?" I shouted after my husband.

"Let it go."

"What if he comes back?" I crossed my arms and clutched my sides. My eyes remained glued to the garbage bag.

My husband shrugged his shoulders. As he approached the woods, two women labored up the hill on their daily walk.

"Good evening ladies, lovely weather."

The taller woman asked, "Whatcha got in that bag?"

"A black snake."

"A what!" said the other woman, staring at the bag with a gaping mouth. "What are you going to do with him?"

"Let it go."

The women's arms powered like chugging locomotives as they climbed the hill's crest and disappeared. My husband set the bag on the ground and jiggled it. "Okay, you're free to go," he said to the snake before he vanished among the leaves.

More frightened than I, the snake had left a foul-smelling musk in the bathtub. That evening I scrubbed with disinfectant until my muscles burned.

For weeks, I tensed every time I pulled back the shower curtain. I was embarrassed to be so scared. My husband said to let it go. That's why I gloated more than you can imagine when I caught him checking the tub too—the snake.

Unwanted Passenger

As gray, breezy, chilly days abate,
Warmer temperatures arrive early
Arouse dormant creatures
I walk in the woods viewing new growth.
Lavender, hairy phlox, golden sundrops,
Wild columbine bob and greet me.
Floral blooms and scents satisfy until

I notice a burnt umber spot on my arm.
    New freckle, NO!
    New age spot, NO!
    New dirt fleck, NO!

Damn, a tick!
YES, a tick!
A tiny, seed tick, barely visible,
An attached poppy seed with six legs.
It's too early for tick larvae.

Returning to my house,
I search for tweezers to remove
The blood-thirsty parasite.
Securely grasp it, extract the pest,
Drop it in a vial of rubbing alcohol, seal,
Wait, hopeful that no Lyme disease or
Rocky Mountain spotted fever
Symptoms will manifest.
A rosy, itching mark
Blazed on my skin, overcome
By a creepy, crawling sensation
Are there more?

Why do ticks even exist?
    To feed chickens and Guinea hens
    To carry viruses and bacteria
    To provide lodging for protozoa
    To control larger host populations
    To annoy and make me sick

If only I could take a tick preventative,
Like my dogs.

Tenacity

"John, it looks like a piece of wiper blade has torn lose." Jennifer said as they cruised south on Interstate 85. "I hope an afternoon thunderstorm doesn't pop up."

"The blades aren't that old. I just had them checked when I had the oil changed last week."

The black band slid up the windshield. Jennifer pressed her feet against the floorboard. She clutched the sides of her seat and scooted back as far as she could. "Oh, shit, it's a snake!" She screamed. She pressed her fingers on the top of the window to make sure it was closed.

The mottled, black snake slithered up the windshield. His muscles contracted. Peering in, he flicked his tongue. Jennifer lowered her chin, clenched her teeth, and clutched her seat tighter. Then she picked up her feet, grabbed her shins, and curled into a ball.

"Calm down. The windows are closed. He'll probably blow off any way," said John.

"I'm not so sure," said Jennifer.

The snake stretched, extended his upper body, and adhered to the windshield as if he had the suction cups of an octopus's tentacle. John remained calm and maintained control of their SUV.

"John, what kind of snake do you think he is?"

"He looks like a harmless, black rat snake. He's a big one. He's got to be at least six feet long."

"I've got to take a picture of him. No one will ever believe us." Jennifer said.

They'd already driven thirty-two miles from their house. The snake maintained his hold. Jennifer eased her clutch, lowered her legs, and settled her feet on the floorboard. Blood flooded back into her fingers. She combed through her pocketbook for her cell phone while she glanced at the snake. She steadied her hands and snapped a photograph of the snake's cream under belly. Then Jennifer switched to video mode as the snake's upper body slid in a fluid motion across the windshield directly in front of her. She winced but held her cell phone firmly. The snake began winding himself around her side mirror. Jennifer cringed. She scooted toward the middle console.

"Jennifer, watch it. You nearly bumped my arm." John said.

"Sorry, sorry, but that snake has wrapped himself around my side mirror." Resembling a ball of black rubber bands, the snake secured his position. "John, I don't think he's going anywhere. Whatever you do, don't open my window. When we get to Durham, I'll get out on your side."

"I'm going to take a slight detour. A park is close by," said John. He turned into the parking lot and chose a spot near the wooded area. "Stay put." He parked, climbed out, and walked around the front of their SUV. The snake's entire body was wound tightly around the passenger side mirror. Sensing the lack of motion, the snake loosened his upper body and flicked his tongue.

"John, be careful. Don't get too close." From safe inside their SUV, Jennifer pointed at the snake's head.

A foot of the snake extended outward, suspended in the air. When he realized he had nothing to climb onto, he retreated to the mirror. John searched for a large, fallen branch. "Maybe I can coax him off."

He nudged the snake, which wriggled, raised his head, and opened his mouth. John stepped back. Then he extended the branch near the snake's head and held the branch steady. The snake inched forward. John knew he couldn't support the snake's entire body, so he carefully propped the free end against their SUV and set his end on the ground. He backed away. Once the snake's upper body reached the ground, Jennifer noticed the tail releasing its grip on the mirror. The snake flicked his tail as he progressed down the branch. John and Jennifer watched as the snake slithered into the grass and wood chips. Once John was back inside their SUV, Jennifer asked, "How did that snake get on our SUV, anyway? We never did figure out how that mouse got inside," said Jennifer.

"It was chilly last night. The snake probably crawled up onto the engine block to get warm. Then this morning as we drove to Durham, the engine block became too hot. With the moving vehicle, he had nowhere to go except out and up onto the windshield." John explained.

"I can't believe he held on for thirty-five miles. It's a good thing you were driving and not me; otherwise, we might have ended up in the ditch." Jennifer said. Furrows formed on Jennifer's forehead, and she pursed her lips. She imagined a sequel, "Skunk in the trunk."

A Garden Visitor's Grievance

My relatives and I live
on every continent except Antarctica,
so why do you accuse me
of being from outer space?
    Is it my stereovision,
    my triangular-shaped head,
    my ability to turn my head 180 degrees?

Are you envious of my slender,
stick-like body or my ability to fly?
Do you wish you, too,
could be a master of disguise?
After all, I allow you
to see me only when I choose.

You say I pray a lot.
If so, my prayer is
I will not fall prey
to bird, bat, lizard, or snake.

My name is a misnomer.
I poise my forearms
equipped with sticky spikes.
A skilled hunter, I wait
silently and patiently
to ambush unsuspecting prey,
like mosquitoes and caterpillars.
Not only am I carnivorous,
but I prefer my meals alive.
I am merciful. I do not
play with my food.

Some view me as a good luck symbol,
but not my mate, whose body
provides me with nourishment.
Others consider me
a spiritual messenger.
I would gladly serve
as a conduit between heaven and earth,
instead, I'll hide contently in your garden.

Not You Again!

While I sit on our sofa
engaged in a suspenseful novel,
you distract me.
Buzz by my shoulder,
seek light and warmth
on your final approach.

Land on the lamp shade,
fold your wings over your back,
like a WWII US Navy "Hellcat" fighter.
Your marbled-brownish, shield-shaped body,
white banded legs and antennae,
make you distinguishable,
a brown marmorated stink bug.

You're not content to stay
outside where you belong,
but you're not welcome in our house.
You dart, bombinate
and constantly annoy me.
Your frass has stained our walls.

Stay still, my grasp will be gentle.
No need to get defensive.
I don't want your foul smell,
secretion lingering on my hands.
I only want to relocate you outside.

Whew, a successful release,
I wash my hands thoroughly,
sit on our sofa
with my novel in hand.
Buzzzzz, not another one!

Precision Pilots

Intrigued by afternoon air show
Like a WWII dog fight
Dive bombing, swerving
Dodging, whizzing by

Aerial acrobatics
Aggressive maneuvering
Territorial challenges over
Precious, cherry-tinted nectar

Iridescent emerald plumage
Shimmering bullets in sunlight
Miniature dare devils
Precision pilots

Circling then touch and go
Quick sip, then zip
Whoosh, hovering
Mid-air refueling

Ruby-throated hummingbirds
Defending critical fuel source

Symphonic Arrival

While the ground is still frosted,
chartreuse leaves punch
through soil and mulch.

An earthy dampness
permeates the spring air.
Silver maple buds awaken.

Warming sun tickles
amethyst and buttercream
crocus blooms.

Listen to the drumming of
pileated, red-headed woodpecker,
honking geese overhead.

A warbler chorus sings their return.
High pitched peepers harmonize.
Honeybees buzz and dance.

As earthworms wriggle upward,
robins hop, peck percussive strikes.
Wind whistles through treetops.

Daffodils, snowdrops, and
hyacinths sway rhythmically.
Concertos inspired by longer days.

Pollinators' Delight

Throughout the year, I anticipate
seed gifts delivered by birds and wind
to our raised flowerbeds.
With spring rains and summer's warmth,

fuzzy, square stems
erupt through the soil.
Narrow foliage bears
deep green, serrated edges.

An unrecognized plant,
I rub and crush a coarse leaf
between my fingers, now stained,
and savor the minty aroma.

Each day I check and recheck for buds,
hopeful for the sight of spectacular blooms
that wave in the breeze like the colorful ribbons
of a rhythmic gymnast.

Days later, lips of lower petals
yield clusters of tubular florets.
Scarlet spikes, brilliant fireworks,
ignite our flowerbeds.

They beckon bees and butterflies.
Hummingbirds hover,
sip sweet nectar,
and tempt me to take a taste.

I gather a bouquet for our table.
The scent of oregano blossoms
permeates the dining room
and complements a meal of pasta.

Thankful for this floral gift
of perennial bee balm.

As the Shield Lifted

After a queen bee's maiden mating flight,
she's confined to the hive to lay eggs,
sheltered in place, caring for the colony.
For the past year, the pandemic restricted me.

Protected from weather and disease,
I sat in our house, read, knitted, and wrote
until my body longed for freedom.
Even a homebody needs to get out now and then.

Drawn curtains obscured the sunlight.
Somber mood shuttered our lives,
stifled creativity, and turned
my writing to macabre script.

My spirit needed warmth and freedom.
I gained temporary salvation
from phone calls, texts, e-mails,
and online meeting videos.

Like a newly hatched bee, emerging from his case,
I flew to town, peered through the car window
at masked and unmasked passersby,
but knew I must return home.

I sat on the porch swing,
listened to the chirps of songbirds, crickets, and toads,
and swayed with zinnias and daisies in the summer breeze
while I learned songs and dances of hope.
Nature was my deliverance.

Remembrance

Ruby-throated hummingbirds,
red admiral butterflies
await warm nectar within
funnel-shaped yellow, orange,
pink gladioli blossoms.

My grandmother's etched glass vase
sits on the dining room table,
awaits her favorite early summer
'Black Star' gladioli with
velvety, maroon blooms
cradled by sword-shaped leaves.

Towering spires with multiple,
colorful blossoms will grace
my flower garden and
complement my grandmother's vase.
Show stopping, spectacular blooms
will eclipse the delicate fragrance.

I sit at the oak table,
sip a cup of hot tea,
picture a freshly cut bouquet.
Short-lived beauties, like Grandma,
remain etched in my memory.

Indispensable Weed

My neighbor complained of
fuzzy, teardrop-shaped pods
atop chartreuse stalks with
paired broad, deep green leaves,
spring, fragrant, white, blush blooms.

"It's an annoying weed,
noxious to my livestock."
Disgruntled, she failed
to understand where
monarchs lay their eggs.

Caterpillars munch only
on milkweed leaves.
Butterflies aren't picky,
sipping wildflowers' nectar,
nourishment among

corridor patches,
steppingstones along
their migratory path.
Eradicate milkweed;
Annihilate monarchs.

Let fall seed pods split open,
so silky-haired seeds can escape,
drift on winds afar—
Perpetuate generations
of monarch butterflies.

Soaring Scavengers

Slightly raised, ebony wings extend
to navigate and maneuver
thermals, columns of warm, rising air.

Wings teeter in silent flight.
Turkey vultures glide to save energy,
always circle clockwise

in coordinated spirals,
like swirling leaves in a wind gust.
Buzzards' kettle towers

soar higher and higher,
periods on azure paper,
indicators of death below.

Misunderstood Fowl

Our dogs barked and barked. Like glowing warning lights, the featherless red heads of two adult turkey vultures, perched on the bare branches of a locust tree beside our driveway. An image of black birds swooping and attacking us and our dogs, like Hitchcock's *The Birds,* unsettled me. I covered my head with my arms and cringed. *Were these birds an omen of death? Is my 91-year-old dad okay?*

I clapped my hands and shouted, shooing the ominous fowl from our dogs' line of vision. The vultures' beady eyes honed on me before they spread their three-foot, dark umber wings and flew toward a dilapidated tobacco barn fifty feet away. Concerned they might return, I scanned our yard for a dead squirrel or rabbit, relieved not to find tempting meals. I bowed my head and sighed. Turkey vultures had circled above fields in our rural neighborhood, but they had never ventured in our yard until now.

After an August afternoon rainstorm, three turkey vultures gather at a puddle in our gravel driveway. One lacks his right foot. *A birth defect or a result of an injury?* I name him Peg Leg. They drink and wade into the muddy water to cool themselves, but they didn't ruffle their feathers and splash.

On an earlier, scorching July afternoon, my daughter and her friends jumped and splashed in a burnt sienna clay puddle. They screamed as they sprayed each other with the garden hose. I shook my head upon seeing their orange-stained bathing suits, but I smiled, enjoying their antics.

The turkey vultures, like the girls, cooled themselves and muddied the water. When the trio of turkey vultures turns their bald heads toward the side porch where I stand, they make no noise. *That's odd.* As I walk toward them, they hobble down the driveway while flapping their wings until they build enough momentum to lift into the air. My muscles relax as they fly away and soar overhead. The contrasts of their awkwardness on the ground with their ease and gracefulness in flight, as well as their silence in my presence, intrigue me. Curiosity replaces my uneasiness. They have no vocal cords, enabling only hisses and grunts. Although I have vocal cords, I don't always voice my feelings. Like vultures, I avoid conflict when possible. Considered non-aggressive fowl, if threatened, they can spew vomit six feet, not something I care to experience. Since learning that, I maintain a respectful distance.

In the evenings, I hear them bang on the rusty tin roof of our tobacco barn. They roost in communal groups. Their hisses alert each other of danger, like roaming coyotes. When I walk our dogs, I tense and increase my gait upon hearing the yips and howls of a coyote pack. My neighbors and I take part in a similar community watch program and call each other if an unfamiliar vehicle lurks along the side of the road. If threatened, I will retreat to safety to call a neighbor or the Granville County sheriff's department. Living in the country has its dangers for people and wildlife, so being vigilant is crucial to staying safe, especially when I ride my bicycle and walk our 2.2-mile block.

Although I don't enjoy huffing and puffing or achy, burning muscles, I relish the aftermath of relaxed, stretched muscles. Like long jump athletes, turkey vultures exert tremendous effort to take flight. While airborne, the birds minimize flapping their wings by riding on thermals, columns of warm rising air. My eyes widen as they glide in spirals, communal groups called kettles, like plumes of black smoke and ash from a volcanic eruption in a cerulean sky. When walking a long distance, I take breaks. Vultures do too. Individuals and small groups rest on posts, utility poles, and exposed tree branches.

Turkey vultures and I enjoy bathing in the afternoon sunlight. Whereas I spread sunscreen on my exposed skin, lie on a beach towel, and laze in the heat; turkey vultures perch and spread their wings in a heraldic stance, slightly raised, to warm themselves, dry their wings, and break off bits of carrion from their featherless heads, necks, legs, and feet. We lock eyes, I smile, they nod, and we bask in the sunlight.

When I get too warm, I go inside; whereas, my bird friends seek shade under our elm trees and sheds. Our feet also regulate our body temperatures. While sleeping, I remove my socks or stick my feet from under the bedsheet until my body cools. In comparison, the vultures urinate or defecate on themselves to cool and sanitize their exposed skin. Although I find uridrosis disgusting, the process provides them comfort and well-being.

Unlike raptors who hunt with their acute eyesight, turkey vultures rely on their keen sense of smell and can detect the sour, garlicky scent of ethyl mercaptan, a gas released by decaying carcasses, up to five miles. They serve as garbage collectors of roadkill. Both of us working to keep our rural community clean, I pick up litter and aluminum cans. These birds are vital to a healthy ecosystem by preventing the spread of diseases, such as botulism, anthrax, and salmonella. Much like my dad, whose cast-iron stomach can handle aged leftovers from the far reaches of his refrigerator, Turkey vultures' powerful bacteria and acids destroy toxic germs and enable them to tolerate others; even their poop is sterile. If only, they'd help me clean the rancid food and gunk from the bowel of our refrigerator.

When I drive county roads, I appreciate their free cleansing service until one hops from a ditch, flaps his wings, and takes too long for lift-off, resulting in a collision with my car's windshield. Thump, crack. I shriek as my fingernails dig into the padded leather steering wheel. Stopping the car, I scan the ground for the wounded bird, hoping I have not hit Peg Leg. I rub my hands and sigh. A handful of feathers sprinkle the rural road. Like a jumbo jet, vultures have a slow, long-distance take-off. Lesson learned. Now, I give them plenty of runway space.

Turkey vultures hold their broad wings with silvery-gray undersides and long finger-like tips in a slight "V" as they soar silently on thermals. Their wings teeter like I did when my parents removed the training wheels from my bicycle. As the bike and I leaned, I squealed; but when I righted the bike, I coasted and giggled. Riding my bike down a hill was the closest I'd come to gliding like a bird with unfurled feathers. I smiled as the air whisked hair from my face.

Misunderstandings occur because of a lack of information or being in the wrong place at the wrong time. When I learned turkey vultures get a negative rap, especially from farmers, who accuse them of killing and devouring newborn lambs, piglets, and calves, I slammed the book closed and clenched my hands. Turkey vultures are social feeders, trailing behind black vultures to consume the disemboweled leftovers, much like hyenas do after a lion kills a zebra or gazelle. *Why are some people so quick to judge?*

In my senior year of high school, two former cheerleaders, who didn't make the varsity squad, accused me of smoking and hoped the administration would remove me from the squad. Punching my pillow as my eyes watered, *why pick on me?* I never smoked, disgusted by my father's smoker's cough, but second-hand smoke sometimes permeated my clothing. Spritzing perfume on my outfits made the aroma worse. Having my senior class advisors, coach, and squad members vouch for me provided reassurance; but the lie hurt, like a hard swallow.

Having relinquished my guilt of having held negative notions about Turkey vultures based on their bald heads, peeing on themselves, and eating dead animals, I advocate for my feathered friends. Like me, people have misunderstood and underestimated the value of these creatures in maintaining a healthy environment. Excluding the residents of Hinckley, Ohio, who celebrate the annual migration of turkey vultures to their town each March, the more I learn about the fowl the greater my appreciation. Why not revere the turkey vulture's role in controlling disease? High time we feature a turkey vulture on a postage stamp.

Backyard Morse Code

I sit on our back deck,
morning coffee cup in hand.
Marshmallow clouds
decorate the cerulean sky.
Sunlight glints through branches.

Scarlet cardinal perches
high on a water elm limb.
His boisterous Morse Code of
dot dash dot dash dot dash
echoes in the morning silence.
Not his usual melodious song of
pretty, pretty, pretty.

What is his urgent message?
    Predator nearby
    Plea for a mate
    Nestlings to feed

I listen and focus
to decipher his message.
Perhaps an SOS,
yet his message fails
to elicit a response.

He flies into the woods.
I stay, finish my coffee,
and shrug my shoulders,
must not have been important.

Where's the Pizza Party?

I know squirrels are clever and resourceful.
Several of my birdfeeders will attest to that.
I guess our neighbor threw out some stale pizza.
Saturday morning a squirrel with a keen sense of smell and
Dexterous paws must have pried open their garbage can,
Retrieving a whole slice of pepperoni pizza.
Then she climbed onto my porch railing, where she sat,
Content with her prized possession
Until another squirrel intended
To sample the tasty treat; but like us,
Squirrels don't always eat what they should,
Nor are they willing to share a special snack.
The squirrel, clasping the pizza slice,
Darted up the closest tree
Hoping to protect her edible treasure.

Hungry Forest Percussionist

A jackhammer perseveres
periodic reverberations
from powerful strikes
upon a decaying elm tree
instead of slabs of concrete

No leaves to buffer the sound
the drumming whack
of a male pileated woodpecker
adorns a flaming red tuft
his mandibular muscles contract

Body absorbs the anvil shock
with each deliberate knock
a skilled excavator
drills for his favorite meal
carpenter ants

Explores with his
protracted, barbed tongue
a series of rectangular holes
among the deep bark ridges
unsuccessful at first
relentless until ants cover his tongue

Solitary Hunters

Autumn morning light bathes the marsh
with a warm calmness. Golden
amber and sienna grasses and reeds
frame a grey heron, a good luck omen.
The beauty of your silhouette casts
upon the glass-like water despite
your disheveled, bristly, ashen feathers
amidst the shallows and stale, musty smell.

I lean forward, hope for a closer view,
watch, listen, alerted by
hoarse, guttural croaks,
a warning or an invitation?
Like you, I enjoy the solitude
of this secluded cove.
We stand portrayed
in a silent movie.

Our senses heightened,
poised for the hunt.
Self-reliant and determined,
armed with your long, sharp beak,
I, with paintbrush and palette.
Your keen eyes scan
beneath the surface
while my eyes search above.

With deliberate steps,
your long, lean legs
wade through the water,
like a downhill skier glides
with ski poles for balance.
I dab paint onto a brush,
place quick strokes on a canvas.
Our swishes synchronize.

Like a driven railroad spike,
you spear a redbreast sunfish.
My eyes sparkle, and
my stomach flutters as
I capture fleeting moments
of light, color, and form.
This intimate place
grounds us.
Patience, skills, and
timing serve us well.
Fish nourishes your hunger
while connecting with
nature feeds mine.

Silent, solitary hunters.

Secluded Berries

Along Caribou Trail within
Coeur d'Alene National Forest,
we search among fir, aspen, and alders
for remote patches of shrubs
that yield plump, round berries.
Our excitement heightens with
the sweet scent of ripe berries.

Black and brown bears forage for
the smaller cousins of blueberries,
western huckleberries,
deep amethyst and sapphire gems,
hide beneath oblong, waxy leaves.

Our bear bells jingle with each step.
Plastic buckets hang around our necks,
swing like pendulums.
Both hands free to pick luscious berries.
Pluck, plop into our buckets.

Unable to resist the juicy berries,
I pop a few in my mouth.
They burst with delicious tartness.
My fingertips wear bluish-red stains.
I dream of huckleberry jam
spread on toasted sourdough bread.

Trapped

Honk, honk! Mandy and Alison scramble to the mountain cabin's picture window. Red wine sloshes in their glasses. Adam and Sean chug their beers and grumble when a referee calls holding against a University of Tennessee linebacker.

"Are you expecting someone else?" asks Alison.

"No, people don't come here unannounced."

Mandy cracks the door. "Hey, Sean, that's your car."

"Probably bumped the key fob in my pocket."

Alison clears her throat. "Again?"

As Sean's fingers fumble the contents of his pants' pocket, loose change jingles. "Oops, must have left it in the car. Be right back."

"Hurry. I came here to relax." Alison holds her left hand to her ear while swigging her wine.

"Here, hold my beer." He dashes to the SUV, but stops when he discerns a massive silhouette in the driver's seat. His muscles tense as the Dodge Durango rocks like a ship in turbulent waters. Gasping with an ashen face, he barges into the living room, but the erratic horn blasts obscure his "damn, help, you won't believe. . . ."

Alison trips and bumps a rocking chair. "What's wrong?"

"Our car, someone's in our car!"

"Out here?" Adam grabs his pump shot gun from the closet and loads two shells.

Mandy clutches her cell phone. "Wait, I'll call the sheriff's office."

"We got this. Sean, come on."

Sean rubs his sweaty palms down his pants' leg. Their wives stand at the door ajar. "Hey, be careful."

Sean nods as Alison gulps her wine and leans against the door frame. Her legs are rubber bands. As Adam and Sean creep toward the SUV, Sean pauses and picks up a baseball bat-sized hickory stick among the fallen leaves. With their mouths gaping, they freeze in front of the vehicle. The semi-fogged windshield obscures their view. Bam, screech! Two-inch long claws smack then etch the glass. Adam and Sean jump. Grunts and bawls, like thunder and gale-force winds, reverberate. A juvenile black bear thrashes and shreds the dashboard before pressing his long snout onto the windshield. Drawing back, Sean wields the stick, wishing he was playing lacrosse rather than confronting a bear. "Hey, get, go on!"

The bear gnaws at the padded steering wheel while the women peer from the door. Alison cuts her eyes toward Mandy. Her lips tremble. Mandy pulls her in for a side hug, spilling her wine. Alison flinches.

"Black bears are typically shy, but I hope you didn't leave any food in the car."

Alsion's forehead furrows. "No, why?"

"Black bears are relentless when food is around."

Alison stares at the SUV. "A raccoon ransacked the garbage cans in our cul de sac. I picked up trash all morning, but a bear."

Sean shrugs his shoulders. "Adam, how the heck did he get in there?"

"You must have left it unlocked, buddy."

"I didn't see the point of locking it way out here."

"Black bears are smart. A few weeks ago, one climbed into a woman's car at Gatlinburg. What a mess!"

Sean's face reddens as he yells and waves the hickory stick. "We've got to get him out before he trashes my Dodge!"

Adam frowns and shakes his head. "Too late, pal."

The bear shreds the seat upholstery, creating a blizzard of padding and foam. While he rummages for food, he discovers a lollipop and plops on the console while holding the sucker between his paws. Sean does a double take, whips out his cell phone, and snaps a photo as the bear extends his tongue and takes a long lick before swallowing the candy, wrapper and all. While resting the shot gun on his left shoulder, Adam pounds one fist on the hood. "Hey, get out of here!"

Is the bear hoping to find more food, or is he trapped, not knowing how to open the door?

Adam signals Sean with a raised open palm, so Sean waits. Hoping the bear will follow him, Adam waves his hands, taps on the glass, and shouts. "Sean, open the driver's door when the bear moves to the rear."

As Sean ducks and slides along the side of the vehicle, he mumbles, "I can do this." The bear charges to the rear, but as Sean approaches the driver's door, the SUV rolls backward.

Mandy and Alison dart onto the porch and lean over the rail. "Watch out!"

Sean hadn't set the emergency brake. The bear must have bumped the gearshift into neutral. Throwing the stick aside, Sean bolts to the front of the SUV, grabs the front bumper, and braces his feet. His heals dig into the gravel, but the vehicle drags him. "Help, I can't hold it." His muscles burn and tremble. He envisions his Durango crashing into a tree and pinning Adam.

The women sprint down the steps and grab the fender on each side of Sean. Within minutes, their fingers cramp, and they let go. Sean's knuckles whiten. Adam leans his shotgun against the woodpile, grabs a hefty log, and lodges it behind the left rear tire. Thump! The SUV jolts, and Sean falls on his butt. Adam darts to the woodpile, snatches another log, and wedges it behind the right rear tire. The bear bounds between the back and front seats, clawing, and jostling the vehicle. "I don't know how long the logs will hold." Adam says as he retrieves the shotgun. Sean winces and brushes the dust from his pants.

Alison's voice quivers. "Are you all right?"

"I'm okay. What about you?"

She wraps her arms around her chest. "A little shaken."

Sean, breathing deeply, strokes her arm. "Go inside. That's one angry bear."

Wringing her hands, Mandy turns to Adam. "You're not going to shoot him, are you?"

"Only if I have to."

The bear slashes the ceiling, and the SUV convulses. The women's eyes widen as they clutch each other's hand and dash to the porch. Adam brings the twelve gauge to his right shoulder, points the barrel at the bear, and pumps the shot gun.

"Sean, go to the driver's door and open it when I say, now."

Glancing toward the SUV, Sean hunches and inches toward the driver's door. With rapid, shallow breaths, he cowers while Adam keeps the bear in his gun sights.

"Now!"

Sean takes a quick breath, pulls the handle, and then crouches behind the door. He clutches his knees and tucks his head, wanting to stay out of the bear's sight. Running could trigger the bear's chase response, and the bear would win this race. When the door opens, the bear raises his head, sniffs the air, and scrambles to the front of the SUV. The bear crawls over the seat onto the ground and stands with his front paws hanging over the door frame. The door bumps Sean's body, and he shudders and moans. Mandy and Alison cling to each other and gasp. Adam yells. The bear shakes his head before bounding toward the woods. Within seconds, he disappears among the forest undergrowth. The women release their hold, and everyone sighs.

Sean braces against the vehicle, stands, slides into the mangled driver's seat, and sets the parking brake. He puts his hand to his mouth and gags from the stench of bear poop. Particles of leather, foam, and plastic litter the vehicle. "Damn, what a mess!" He slams the ripped steering wheel. "Totaled." As Sean climbs from the SUV,

Mandy and Alison scan the yard and then hustle to their husbands.

Adam says, "I didn't know who was scared more, Sean or the bear?" After unloading the shot gun, he chuckles as he reaches for the shells on the ground. "You okay?"

Sean nods and sighs as his shoulders slump. Alison rubs his back. "Sure, you're okay?"

"Yeah, but it's going to be one uncomfortable ride home, but I'll have one heck of a story to tell."

Vigilant Hunter

Harsh, discordant pitch
Distant screech like fabric ribbing
Red-tailed hawk soars high
Above freshly mowed wheat field
Methodical, slow, deep beats
Of wings spanning three feet
Like the drums of warriors
Signaling the hunt
One pass, two passes
Focused, keen eyes
Scour for a field mouse
Fallen wheat chaff twitches
Rufous feathers skim the surface
Sharp talons poised
Swoops down, snatches her prey
Clutches, tightening vice grip
Ascends to upper oak branch
To devour her meal
Vigilant observer
Remains perched

Amber Eyes

Leah looked forward to another relaxing night walk with her border collie, Molly, down the long, rural driveway. The air was crisp and still. Their arthritic joints dictated a slow pace. As they walked beneath the dusk to dawn light, a bat darted after a luna moth drawn to the bulb. Leah ducked and flung one arm over her head instinctively. Each time Molly paused to mark her territory; Leah looked up at the clear sky. "Look Molly, there's the Big Dipper and the Little Dipper. Now, if I could just find Orion." Molly sniffed the ground.

When they reached the end of the driveway, Molly tugged on the leash, seeking to walk farther. "Molly, no. Time to go back." The high-pitched, piercing howls and barks of a pack of coyotes sliced through the still air. Leah had heard the lonely howl of a single coyote before, but she had never heard the blood curdling cries of a coyote pack. Leah flinched then froze. Her muscles tightened, and her arm hair rose. She pulled Molly close to her side. Molly's back fur bristled, and she growled. "Molly, hush. Stay." Leah wished they could become invisible.

Leah knew coyotes were usually timid and fearful of people, but she didn't know how a pack would behave. She'd heard they could take down a white-tailed deer. *I only weigh 112 pounds, and Molly is only thirty-five pounds. A pack could easily take us down.* Leah shuddered at the thought, and her heart raced. She couldn't tell if the coyotes were in the woods or the field across the road. She held the flashlight in her trembling left hand and did a panoramic sweep of the field. She almost dropped the flashlight when she saw four sets of glowing, amber eyes. Who was more afraid, Leah or the coyotes?

Molly kept growling and jerking forward. Leah gripped the leash so tightly that her fingers went numb. She wanted to run, but her legs wouldn't move. Just as well, she feared the coyotes would chase after them, and she knew they couldn't outrun them. "Molly hush, stay still." Leah grabbed Molly's collar. "Hush, girl." If only she could get Molly quiet, may be the coyotes would move on to another field. Leah was shaking, not knowing what the pack would do. Molly kept barking. Amber eyes kept staring. Were the coyotes trying to anticipate her next move? It was like playing a game of "Chicken."

Molly barked and lunged again. Leah's fingers slipped from Molly's collar. She clutched Molly's leash. Unsure what to do, Leah shouted, whistled, and waved the flashlight. She kicked up some gravel. She hoped she could intimidate the coyotes. After a few minutes, the amber eyes disappeared in the tall grass. Leah bent and gasped. Her heart still raced. Molly continued barking then raised her head and sniffed the air. Leah patted her on the head to reassure them both.

Leah composed herself as best she could. "Molly, let's go." Before turning around, Leah took a few steps backward. She shone the flashlight and scanned the field. "Are they really gone, girl?"
Molly sniffed the air. "Okay, let's go." Leah and Molly's pace quickened the closer they got to the house. Once on the porch, Leah stopped and listened, but all she heard was Molly panting and her own rapid, shallow breathing.

Now safe inside, Leah detached Molly's leash. Molly stood guard at the door while Leah fixed herself a cup of a hot chamomile tea. Leah sat on the couch and sipped the tea trying to calm down. "We're all right now, girl. Just relax." Molly curled up on the rug at Leah's feet.

Leah longed for a quiet night's sleep. She was relieved to hear only the sonorous hoots of a great horned owl and Molly's soft snores.

The next day Leah shared her unnerving experience with a friend. "Coyotes make an awful racket when it's mating season. Sound like a bunch of wild cats dying," said Leonard.

"No more nightly walks for us, Molly. We'll wait until mating season is over."

Molly cocked her head in agreement.

Nocturnal Prowess

Late last night, shrieks and squawks
from the chicken coop, pierced
the night, awakened neighbors.

Torn screen, maimed chickens,
broken eggs strewn across the yard.
Neighbors, not knowing which culprits:
red fox, raccoon, opossum to blame.

Coyotes' distant howls grew
closer as their habitat's destroyed
by local timbering and construction.

The next morning I drove our country road,
the sun rose above the trees,
an animal posed on the center yellow line.
The car slowed, rolled closer, and then stopped.

I leaned against the steering wheel,
eyes widened and mouth gaped
at my first sighting of a solitary bobcat.

His white fur lining highlighted amber eyes.
Ebony rosettes marked his tan coat.
Black, tufted ears with white centers
listened for movement.

The bobcat with ruffed cheeks turned his head.
For a fleeting moment our eyes met
and shared a respectful glance.

Before the cat darted into the brush,
his bobbed, black-tipped tail barely visible.
I sat and sighed, hoping
the elusive feline would reappear.

Now more committed,
I pledged to preserve
our woods.

Escapee

When I arrived twelve days ago, I cowered in a corner, but now my paws ache from pacing in this confined space among strangers. I can't stand another night of the howling beagle, causing my hair to spike and my head to throb.

On this sweltering evening, when an assistant brings my dinner, I ignore him. He coaxes me to eat by holding a chunk of tuna in his extended fingers. My empty, queasy stomach gurgles. The tuna smells delicious, but when he bends and slides the dish toward me, I bolt through the open door. He turns too slowly to grab me. I hide, trembling behind a bush, before climbing a nearby tree. I hold my breath as the assistant combs the bushes. "Tony, where the heck are you?"

I don't want to get him in trouble, but I want my freedom. He scours the grounds with a flashlight for twenty minutes, and then he quits. "Stay put. I'll find you in the morning." Finding a sturdy branch, I drape my legs like a tossed bean bag, doze, and dream of my adventure home.

At first light before his search resumes, I clutch the rough bark and back down the trunk. Romping with my head held high, I smell roadside honeysuckle and wild buttercups until I choke on the exhaust fumes of passing cars. Honk, honk. A pickup truck swerves. My pulse races as I dart into the tall grass, hoping the road crew won't mow today. My stomach growls. Blades of grass wave while I forage. A cricket jumps. My tail twitches as I crouch and focus. Pouncing, I close my front paws around the cricket, but the insect slips through them. On my next hunt, I capture a grasshopper, a crunchy treat, but I yearn for a tasty field mouse.

Surely, I'll be home by nightfall; but when twilight arrives, I reach the edge of town with rows of houses and well-manicured yards. When a siren blares, my hair ruffles, and my ears hurt. I dodge among pedestrians carrying shopping bags while cars whizz through the town. As I dash across the street, a blue sedan's brakes squeal. Gasping, I scramble to the curb and then scurry into an alley.

My nostrils flare with the smell of fish wafting through the evening air. I cock my head, my mouth waters, and my stomach churns. Following the scent into the alley, I discover a dumpster. Although I jumped from the floor to my owner's dining room table, I could never jump high enough to get into the dumpster. If I climb in, I might not get out, trapped again. I meow at the back door, hoping a cook or waiter will toss me a food scrap. My nails screech and etch the back door. I yowl. A towering man, wearing a spattered white apron and waving a shiny object, comes to the door. "Get, go on. Get out of here."

I quiver and duck behind the dumpster. Once he closes the door, I wait and try again. My hunger overpowers me, so I wail until a young man comes to the door. He holds a can and mumbles to himself. "Hey, I bet you want something to eat. Hold on, I'll see what I can find." He returns with a small saucer of milk and a chicken wing. I rub against his leg to show my approval, and then I lap the milk and gnaw the chicken from the bone. Now, I need a safe, quiet place to spend the night.

As I ramble through the alley, a raggedy black cat prowls. He growls and hisses, arching his back and puffing his fur. His tail thrashes back and forth. *I get the message; I am trespassing.* I hiss and spit, hoping he'll stand down, because I am too tired to fight. Swallowing my pride, I dart past him. He spits, swats, and chases me to the end of the alley.

Panting, I follow the main street to a central park with a water tower, oak trees, and wooden benches. As I trot along the sidewalk, a barking Doberman pinscher pursues me and nips my tail.

Screaming, I twist and slash a front claw across his face. He howls but then slaps a paw on my back, knocking me to the ground. I kick and squirm, avoiding his gnashing teeth. When I bite his paw, I wiggle free, dash to the base of a tree, and climb to a hefty limb. I moan and lick my scrapes. The dog barks and lunges at the tree trunk. When my hind leg slips, I wobble and clutch the branch. Soon, the dog's owner harnesses him, tugs the leash, and walks away. As the barking fades, I sprawl across the branch and sigh.

At dawn, I scoot down the tree in search of food and arrive at a brick house on the corner. The house is dark and quiet, so I scrounge for scraps at the garbage cans, where I find a crusty, greasy slice of anchovy pizza. While chewing an anchovy, I choke, and my eyes water. Next, I gobble the stale cheese before sauntering to the end of the street.

Sniffing the ground, I step across the field of freshly cut grass, sprinkled with morning dew, and then shake my paws. If I don't get home soon, my family, assuming I'm lost or dead, will get another cat. Sharing with the family dog is enough. Cans and wrappers litter the bleachers at the edge of the field. I flick my paw to release a sticky candy wrapper. A stained sweatshirt beneath the bleachers provides a secure hiding and resting place during the scorching day.

That night, relying on my sense of smell and instinct, I hike through the woods. When three cats with scarred faces and matted fur approach, I withdraw behind a tree. I pant and salivate.

"Come join us," says the calico cat. They smirk.

Perhaps they can guide me through the woods. Within minutes of joining them, they swat each other, arguing about which way to go and complaining of hunger. I paw my ears and shake my head.

Preferring my solitude and hoping the scruffy trio will leave me alone, I say good-bye and creep in the opposite direction. My fur bristles as the thick undergrowth brushes my body. Briars stick to my coat, and vines wrap around my legs like the tentacles of an octopus. Thorny, wild blackberries prick my skin. I zigzag and crawl. "Me-ow, ow!" With my teeth, I pluck a thorn from my tattered tail. My red, tender paw pads burn. Licking them, I taste blood and spit.

Amidst looming shadows, I crouch and tiptoe. A low hoot shifts to a high shrill. *Is an owl or a bobcat hunting?* My ears twitch while I lower my tail and slink. Whoosh, my back hairs bristle as I scoot toward a bush. Too late, a huge owl's talons thrust into my skin and lift my body. Screaming and writhing, I plunge to the ground. The owl carries away a tuft of gray fur. "Meow, meow!" I squirm under a bush and wait until the owl swoops to a distant tree. Peering from the bush, I lurk through the groundcover. *What happened to my free-spirited adventure?*

When I arrive at the creek, no bridge is in sight, so I trudge along the water's edge. The creek is too wide to cross unless I find a fallen tree or stepping rocks. My stomach contracts with hunger pangs. A crayfish flutters in the shallows. I pounce, catching him in my claws and teeth. Crunch. As I bend to slurp the water, air bubbles float to the surface. When I slip and fall into the creek, the pointy nose of a snapping turtle emerges. I scramble, splash, and hiss. After I reach a safe distance, I shake my head and paws and then crawl parallel to the creek bed.

Thud, thud, thud. My ears lift while a vehicle rumbles over the bridge with towering rusty, metal girders. I claw up the steep bank onto the one lane bridge. Although I want to get home, my legs and paws throb. A farmhouse and dilapidated barn stand within sight of the bridge. I drag to the barn, where a bulb buzzes and flickers.

Moths hover in the light beam, too high to swat. Squeezing through a crack in the wooden planks, I lug myself onto a straw bale, collapse, and curl my body. *I'm dying.*

When the morning sunlight shines through a ceiling crack, I wake and stretch my legs, but my legs cramp, and I cry. *How will I get home?* Rubbing my legs helps relieve the muscle spasms. My desire to be with my family propels me from bale to bale until I slide onto the dirt floor. Then I shimmy through a slit between the rotting boards. Someone stapled a photograph of a cat to a pole. After squinting at the faded photograph, I moisten my paws and stroke my face. My body fights gravity as I labor to lift my legs. While I clamber the hill, I stumble and tumble several feet. Dazed, I flounder, before proceeding.

At the crest, my body crumples, and my heart pounds. Gasping, I limp along the lane until I arrive at the house with the ceramic gnomes in the flowerbeds. I struggle across the neighbors' yard to the overgrown hedge row with bluish-purple berries that separates their backyard from my owners'. After crossing the backyards, I crawl to my family's porch. With labored breath, I wail, "Let me in." My battered body with protruding ribs topples against the metal screen door. Thunk.

A glimmer of light shines through the kitchen window, and my ears perk to a familiar voice. "Mom, Dad, Something's at the back door." Suzy cracks the door and yells. "It's Tony. It's Tony. He's home!" She props the door with her foot, reaches, and cuddles me in her arms. I squirm. Although scabs cover my scratches, my sores hurt.

"Mom, Dad, Tony's hurt."

Suzy's dad tells her to set me on the kitchen floor. I groan and wince while he rubs his hands over my body, feeling for injuries. "His scratches are superficial."

"He's so skinny." Her voice quavers, and her eyes water.

"Give him some food and let him rest."

"Dad, are you sure he's all right?"

"If he doesn't eat, we'll have Dr. Hadley check him."

No, way! I'm not going to the vet's and be confined again. Suzy brings my favorite meal, so I lap the milk and nibble the tuna chunks. Too weak to wash my paws and whiskers, Suzy dabs them with a warm, damp washcloth. When she nestles me in my bed, I nuzzle my head against her arm. While she picks the burs from my matted fur, I flinch. After she finishes, I purr. As she strokes my back and says, "Don't worry; I'll take care of you," my muscles relax, and I drift to sleep, dreaming of catnip treats.

Beaver Moon

Before the hard frost crystalizes dewy grass
and ice coats the pond, bundled in my parka
I venture out on a chilly November night.

Gnawed and felled birch and willow trees,
evidence of your presence, line the winding trail,
yet you elude my attempts to watch you work.

The full frost moon lights my path
and shimmers on the murky water.
I stand at the shore and scan the surface.

My eyes spot movement and follow
ripples that lead to your dark, brown head.
Your body glides through the water.

You dive and disappear
into your domed, wooden lodge,
a signal for me to go home too.

The beaver moon guides me.
Your presence, a gift this night.

Mitzi

Mitzi, my loyal English pointer,
each day after work you greeted me
with exuberant barks and tail wags.
You stood by me, reached to my mid-thigh.

Your body far leaner and more muscular than mine.
Like dedicated Olympians, we trained together,
eager to hunt game birds whenever I called you
with one short blast of my whistle.

You sported a camouflage of
brown spots on cream-colored short hair
while I wore my orange hat and vest.
We tramped through grain fields.

Sometimes you disappeared.
I scanned the field, gave two
loud whistles, and up you
jumped for me to see you.

With neck stretched forward,
your keen snout sniffed the air
for the scent of well-hidden birds.
Once detected, you went on point with grace.

Your eyes focused ahead,
one front leg bent at a right angle,
poised, elongated body and straight tail,
an arrow honed on its target.

We flushed out birds; they flew.
I raised and fired my shotgun.
You never flinched or wavered,
patiently you waited for my command.

I clapped my hands,
your signal to fetch.
Alert, persistent, you retrieved a quail,
gently mouthed her as you ran back to me.

Proud of your find,
you dropped her at my feet.
I patted your head, "Good girl."
You wagged your tail in agreement.

Horizontal wave of my flat hand,
you lay down, a deserved rest.
No better hunting partner did I have
than you, my trusted friend.

Beacon

January evening walk with Bear,
our shepherd-Labrador mix,
full moon lights our path.

Arctic gusts shove us along,
our strides keep up with
lengthening shadows.

Our breaths form clouds.
Bundled up in heavy coats,
exposed skin stings.

Shivering branches wave,
wind whistles, a signal
that hurries us on our walk.

Frosted sweet gum leaves, scattered
starfish glisten. Seed balls tumble
like sea urchin in the surf.

I long for barefoot massages
on warm, white, sandy beaches.
Instead, my clunky boots

traverse uneven, frozen
ground. The iced moon serves
as our beacon back home.

Rescued Dog and a Poet

Lost or abandoned, you
found your way down a
long, gravel driveway in
rural Piedmont North Carolina.

We rescued each other with
mutual love and respect.
You gave me more.
Rescued me from writing

mundane material.
I could have taught you to
retrieve my slippers or
fetch the newspaper.

You provided a different service.
Your sensitive nose, ears, and eyes
guided me to keen observations.

I looked on the ground,
you uncovered a mud turtle.
A poem surfaced.

    Umber dome lay still
    Left undisturbed like a rock
    Till dog caught its scent

I looked into the treetops.
You spotted a groundhog.
A story emerged.

    Startled by barking dogs,
    a groundhog climbed the tree trunk.
    Then he rested in the fork of two branches.

On our walks, ideas sprang forth.
Back home, I set pen to paper,
captured my thoughts and observations.
Thanks to you, I am more
connected to our natural world.

Minuscule Moments

You're comfortable in your pack
and I in my circle of friends.
Over time, our energy wanes.

We seek the alone stillness within my study.
I sit at my oak desk before a window.
You sit to my right upon a wing chair.

No words are spoken.
No sounds are made
beyond our breaths and heart beats.

I raise my hand to my chin,
draw my pen to my lips.
You are ready to listen to
my thoughts and scribbles.

I contemplate how to begin as if
I expect you to offer a suggestion.
I tap my pen, you wag your tail
in synchronization.

Iridescent hummingbird darts past
then alights on an elm branch.
I smile and write, "minuscule."

What's the significance of a blink,
freckle, seed, tear, flea?
You bark, "toasted oats, mini-marshmallow treats."

Mother's Day Dilemma

The house lights flickered. The wind roared and thunder clapped and boomed. The Cottrell's dogs barked an alarm from their dog houses. Sara pulled back the curtains and stared out the window as raindrops pelted the glass. "I can't see anything. What's upsetting Nikki and Bear? Every ten minutes, Sara dashed over to the side door, listened, and looked. They heard no thunder, nor did they see lightning reflected through the windows for thirty minutes. Her mom conceded to let her check on their dogs, so Sara pulled on her raincoat and boots.

"Don't stay long. I'll have a towel ready."

Holding a flashlight, Sara walked down the slick, wooden steps. Nikki and Bear poked their heads from their dog houses and looked toward the teal sedan. Sara searched around the car as raindrops dripped in her eyes. "What's wrong? What do you smell?" She crouched and shone the flashlight under the car. Amber eyes reflected the light, and then she heard an animal whimpering.

"Don't move. I'll be back." She dashed and slipped. When she caught herself, her right knee hit the top step. "Ouch!" She dropped the flashlight, which rolled across the porch.

Hearing a thunk, her mother rushed and opened the door as Sara pulled herself up. "Are you okay?"

"Mom, Dad, an animal is under the car. Sounded like a puppy."

"So that's why the dogs are barking," said her dad.

"I need your help. I can't reach him."

Her parents threw on their raincoats and boots, and her dad pulled on heavy work gloves. "He's scared and might bite."

Her mom held a flashlight while her dad reached under the far side of the car. "Sara, see if you can calm Nikki and Bear."

"Shhh, it's okay." They continued to bark.

"I'm getting too old for this," her dad moaned as his elbows scraped the gravel. "I can't reach him, and he's not budging."

"Sara, go get a dog treat and a towel. May be we can coax him out," said her mom.

Sara returned, squatted, and held the treat under the car. "Come on, little buddy. I won't hurt you." The puppy inched forward, growled, and then cowered. Sara scooted on her stomach. "Buddy, come on. Look, I have a treat." The puppy crawled forward and latched onto the chew treat. Sara reached around with her other arm and pulled the puppy to her.

"Be careful." Her dad said.

"Dad, I know. Mom, he's shaking."

"Wrap him in the towel; we'll clean him inside."

The puppy crouched in the towel while Sara held him to her chest. As they stood in the kitchen, water pooled on the linoleum floor. "Don't move. I'll get more towels," said her mom.

Upon closer inspection, ticks and fleas covered the beagle mix puppy with a scrape on his nose. "Why do emergencies have to happen on weekends?" Sara's mom called an emergency animal clinic in Durham, North Carolina. "We've got to leave right now. The vet has agreed to see us."

When they arrived at 9 PM, a vet technician unlocked the door. "What have you got there?"

Sara extended her arms. The puppy's nose protruded from the towel.

"I'll take him. Where did you find him?"

"Under our car," said Sara. "Will he be all right?"

"Dr. Saber will exam him and will let you know."

After twenty minutes, Dr. Saber entered the waiting room. "I'd guess he's two or three months old. He's anemic from the tick and flea bites. We gave him a flea dip, but we had to pick off most of the ticks. He should be okay. Do you plan to keep him?"

"Can we, Dad? He's so cute."

"No, we have two dogs. That's enough. I'm sure they can find him a good home."

Sara stuck out her lower lip and hung her head. "Please, Dad, Mom!"

Dr. Saber pointed to the front desk. "Anita will explain the charges and answer any questions."

"Thank you."

After Anita explained the charges, Sara's dad turned and said, "Well, if I've got to spend that much, I guess we'll be a three-dog family." He turned to his wife. "Happy Mother's Day."

Sara smiled and hugged her dad. "Can he be my dog?"

"Ask your mom, he's her Mother's Day gift."

"Mom, can I?"

"Yes, but you'll have to take care of him."

"What should we call him?"

"Well you've been calling him Buddy all night." Her dad said.

"Okay, he kinda looks like a Buddy." Sara nodded.

The vet technician placed the puppy, wrapped in a dry warm towel, in Sara's open arms. Sara gave him a hug and whispered, "Buddy, you're going home."

My Guardian

Buddy, I cannot smell your essence,
only where you have been and
what you have done—
rolled in freshly cut grass,
jumped in the farm pond.

You sniff and know
my unique scent,
my molecular being.

You identify each ingredient
as though I am a bowl of stew.
I cannot hide my emotions,
my health issues from you.
My private diagnostician,

You determine what I need:
furry snuggle for reassurance,
gentle nudge to say, "Let's go."

You understand me.
I wish I could reciprocate
beyond, a pat on the head,
"Good dog," or "Here's a treat."

You speak. I look, I listen,
I make my best guess
without a keen sense of
smell to guide me.

You wait. You cock your head.
Stare with your amber eyes.
When will she figure it out?
You sit patiently. You try again.

You fetch your leash,
wag your white-tipped tail.
Our love extends
beyond companionship,
my guardian, Buddy.

Up a Tree

Hearing our dogs' rapid, low-pitched barks, my muscles tense, and I turn to my husband. "Please see what's wrong."

My husband opens the side door. "Hey, what are you barking at?"

Is a skunk returning to dig for grubs in our yard on this sunny autumn afternoon? My husband fails to scrunch his nose or rub his eyes, so the skunk's repugnant spray from last night has dissipated. Thank goodness the skunk didn't spray our dogs. My husband returns, shaking his head. "I don't know why they're upset. Nothing unusual, two squirrels are chasing each other around the elm trees."

"Maybe they're complaining about the white barn cat. She sits in our driveway and taunts them."

"Nope, didn't see the cat or hear other dogs."

"Okay, but something's wrong. They must smell another animal or maybe a person." In a recent issue of our local newspaper, I read about break-ins five miles from our house. I can't ignore our dogs' barking, but I hesitate going outside.

Rubbing his head and glaring at me, my husband plops on the sofa, reaches for his headphones, and sets his computer in his lap. *He's done.*

After peering through the side door window, I lurk toward their kennels. I stay close to our dogs in case someone is nearby. "Calm down; what's wrong?" I say in my most soothing voice while reaching my hand through the metal-linked fence to pet Buddy and Beau. Despite my efforts to reassure them, they pace, bark, and growl as they gaze at the tree line. When they do pause, I hear no rustling in the bushes or sticks cracking under foot.

Scanning our yard, driveway, and the edge of the woods, no sign of white-tailed deer, raccoon, or wild turkey is apparent. A sparrow flies and perches on the birdbath. Buddy and Beau stand with ruffled fur on their backs and stick their noses through the kennel fence. Bear tilts her head, resembling the RCA Victrola dog. Expecting to see an opossum, I squint and focus my attention on the closest line of trees, but I see nothing strange among the russet foliage.

"Beau, what do you see?" I wait and rub my hands. He runs in a circle, then sits with his head cocked upward, and sniffs the air. Bear and Buddy woof in rapid succession. A breeze carries a musky scent that permeates my nostrils. I stroke the back of my neck. While my eyes follow Beau's gaze, I peer at a large elm tree near the fence line. Straining my neck for a closer look, I spot a small, plump animal with dark brown, bristly fur and a short bushy tail twitching, but the creature isn't a raccoon or a squirrel. The broad, flat head resembles a groundhog. My eyes widen. *It can't be! Groundhogs don't climb trees.*

The groundhog lies with his belly wedged in the fork of two large branches about twenty feet above the ground. *Is the animal sleeping, hurt, scared?* Our dogs pace and bark. "Calm down." I wave my hands at them, but they ignore me. I dash to the house and tap my husband on the arm. He jerks. "Napping again?"

"What? No, resting my eyes. Did you figure out why they're barking?"

"Hurry, you've got to see this; you won't believe it." I wait at the door while my husband whips off the headphones, sets the computer aside, and grabs his shoes. He follows me to the base of the elm tree, where I point toward the fork in the tree. "Look, he's still there."

"Hey, isn't that a groundhog? I didn't know they could climb trees."

"Neither did I, but there he is. Do you think he's okay?"

"I hope so. The county animal control won't come to get him."

The groundhog turns his head. I jump, expecting him to bare his teeth, but he remains still.

"Do groundhogs get rabies?" I shudder. A few years ago, we suspected a rabid raccoon when he darted in and out of the woods during the day although I never got close enough to see foaming around his mouth. Two days later, I found him dead, curled at the base of our mailbox. "You're not going to try to get him down, are you? He might bite, or more likely, you'll fall."

"No, I don't have a ladder tall enough."

The groundhog's stubby legs sprawl over the branches as he rests comfortably. Upon our acknowledgment of the uninvited napper, our dogs calm and lie at the entrances to their dog houses. While keeping wary eyes on us, they wait for us to remove the intruder.

"Do you think the groundhog will climb down?"

"He climbed the tree, so he can get down. I bet the groundhog found some corn kernels left by the deer, and then our dogs scared him."

"But where did he come from? I've never seen a groundhog on our property."

"With the crops and vegetable gardens around here, they're close by."

"Keep an eye on him. I'll be right back; I want to get my camera and take a picture." Our friends won't believe this unless I have proof. When I return, our dogs stand at attention. Positioned beneath the forked branch, I shift my weight from side to side, but I can't see his head. My husband nudges my right arm.

"Don't startle him. We don't want him to climb higher."

I take three full breaths before I focus the lens and snap two photographs.

"Did you get him?"

"I think so, but he's well-camouflaged." I tuck my camera into my pocket, and then my husband and I walk to our dogs' kennels.

He pets Bear, and I pat Buddy's and Beau's heads. "Good dogs. Thank you." Knowing our dogs will alert us to any uninvited visitors, curiosity replaces my uneasiness.

We return to our living room, hoping our dogs will remain calm, so the groundhog will leave. While waiting, I research rodents on my computer and learn that groundhogs with their short, muscular legs and clawed toes can climb trees and swim. A YouTube video, providing additional proof, shows a groundhog scrambling up a tree trunk. If tree climbing is common among groundhogs, why hasn't my husband or I ever heard of it? We have seen them on the side of the road, munching grass or standing alert, but we've never seen one in a tree.

That evening after we throw corn kernels for the deer, we walk to the large elm tree, where we'd seen the groundhog. Not only has he disappeared, but we never see him again. Our dogs curl and nap on the cedar shavings until the next uninvited guest arrives.

Mutual Observers

The glint of an ebony jewelwing
damselfly's iridescent, emerald body
like the green flash the moment
the sun's upper rim dips below
the horizon attracts our attention.
His slender body glistens,
resembles the shimmer of the last day's
sunlight on the ocean.
The veins within his broad,
cobalt wings resemble the rigging
on a schooner with hoisted sails.

The damselfly slices
through summer's heavy air
like a ship's hull plows
through turbulent waters.
The jewelwing flits among sun-dappled leaves
along the shallow creek
that meanders through the woods.

Poised with his wings above his back,
the damselfly rests on a low-lying
glossy, green mayapple leaf.
We sit upon a fallen branch
and observe the still insect.
He watches us with pronounced eyes,
and then snaps his wings
as if to say, "Good morning."

Garden Guardians

Colonies of ladybugs seek shelter
from wintry weather, decorate our ceilings,
huddle in corners for warmth.

Confused by a warm November day,
a multitude of ladybugs appear,
paint our house red and black.

Beetles of our Lady, the Virgin Mary,
don a red cloak, black spots
symbolize her joys and sorrows.

Aphids and mites plagued fields,
ravaged annual crops of wheat and barley.
Livestock hungered, and famine ensued.

The Virgin Mary answered prayers
of Medieval farmers by sending tiny beetles,
purposed with devouring pests.

Ladybugs endure fall and winter.
We welcome them each spring
as guardians of our garden.

Avian Immersion

Hidden jewels lie within
Sylvan Heights Bird Park.
Teal ducks, mallards, swans, and geese
paddle, glide, and ripple the water.
Carp swim and hide in the shadows.
Painted turtles sunbath on floating logs
within the fountained central pond.
Wind shifts, sprays onlookers, no complaints
on this sultry summer day.

We embark on winding pathways
to view rare and exotic waterfowl,
like white-winged wood ducks and
ruddy-headed geese, as well as
more common birds representing six continents.

We walk through aviaries of parrots, macaws,
toucans. Pause to view scarlet ibis, spoonbills
as hummingbirds dart from blossom to blossom.
Admire the colorful and iridescent plumage.

After we purchase a seed stick and food pellet bag,
we enter the feeding station, not for timid observers,
as parakeets alight on hands, arms, shoulders, and heads.
Birds tickle our skin and ruffle our hair.
We stand motionless. Most snack on seeds
while others nibble on jewelry and shoelaces.
Some visitors choose to feed the more subdued flamingos.

Throughout the park, we listen to the cacophony
of caws, honks, screeches, and squawks
until melodious songs delight our ears,
immersed in an ornithological paradise.

Short Poems

Ground begins to thaw.
Peepers courting serenade
Within damp grasses.

Spring peepers emerge,
Deafening symphonic trills
As temperatures warm.

March courtships echo—
Barred owls hoot, woodpeckers drum,
Songbirds chirp in woods.

Chirping spring peepers
Bullfrog's deep guttural croaks
Silenced by the wind

Backyard visitors
Skunks persistently digging
Spring's harvest of grubs

Nature's miniature
Hovering helicopters
Seeking one more sip

Spontaneous flight
Black starlings' murmuration
Flocking to the trees

Sultry summer's night
Crickets and tree frogs chirping
Deafening at times

Silenced by footsteps
Peepers' undisclosed secrets
Patiently, I wait

Great horned owl wakens.
Low, sonorous hoots resound,
Haunt the night forest.

Silent twilight flight
Talons and shrieks pierce stale air
Fluff flies, my eyes tear

Rat-a-tat-tat
One of nature's musicians
In search of insects

Scampering chipmunk
Chubby cheeks stuffed with acorns
Fall preparation

Coyote presence
Gone are the coveys of quail
Missing Bob White calls

Nightly woods' silence
Great horned owl's interruptions
Deep, serial hoots

Grazing in Yellowstone
Wild buffalo herds
Symbols of times past

Newly fallen snow
Reveals late night visitors
Silent footprints rest

Egrets

Tucked beneath their wings
Tree napping at water's edge
Moonlit silhouettes

Thoroughbred

Ears perked, nostrils flared
Airborne, a fleeting moment
Racing like the wind

Nightly Eye Shine

Night
cold grass
green eye shine,
Carolina wolf spiders
hunting crickets.

Longing for Your Call

My ears long for the cheerful whistle of "bob-white" on warm
        evenings
Instead I hear the encroaching, whining howl of coyotes

Missed are your quail coveys in the fall and winter
And your solitary pairs in spring and summer
Occasionally glimpsed in the brush
Served well by your mottled
Russet plumage camouflage

Once you indulged in fields of soybeans and sorghum
Once you consumed ragweed and foxtail grass seeds

Masters at hiding until startled
Then flushed into hasty flight
Escaping only to scurry for cover
Roosting nightly in compact circles, heads turned out
Vigilant for communal protection

Having chosen not to migrate
I am saddened by your dwindling numbers

Your hedge rows are now barbed wire fences
Your fields reduced to corn and alfalfa
Your woodlands are timbered
Raccoons and snakes rob your nests of eggs
Predators threaten your members

The mournful silence is
A reminder of what's been lost

Unexpected Visitors

As my husband and I drove through the Texas Panhandle, the bobbing and clacking of the pump jacks, oil derricks, greeted us. Long-horn steer grazed along miles and miles of fence line. The sparse, windswept vegetation of scrubby, dwarf junipers and mesquite, buffalo grass, and prickly pear, and yucca cacti was a stark difference from the abundant green vegetation of Piedmont North Carolina. Occasionally a piece of tumbleweed rolled across the highway. The land appeared barren, harsh, and uninviting.

We checked in at the rangers' station at the entrance to Palo Duro Canyon State Park, not too far from Amarillo, Texas, and examined the park map. We hadn't realized previously that Palo Duro Canyon was the second largest canyon in the United States. We drove down to our primitive campsite in the Cactus Camp Area for the night. Our car thermometer read 105 degrees. When we stepped out of our car, the dry heat smacked us in the face. Static electrified my fly away hair. I unsuccessfully brushed the clinging hair out of my face; I quickly felt parched and coated with dust.

We unloaded only the essential camping gear for our one night stay. We set up our tent and cots for our sleeping bags. I recalled the park ranger's unsettling advice, "I do not recommend sleeping on the ground. Remember to shake out your shoes in the morning before you put them on." My arm hairs bristled, and my muscles tensed as I thought about the possibility of unwanted visitors, western diamondback rattlesnakes and scorpions. I questioned our decision to camp here rather than stay at a hotel in Amarillo, but we were trying to save money. *What were we thinking? Calm down. What are the chances of undesirable visitors? I can do this. I've always enjoyed camping. This will be another adventure.*

We climbed on the concrete picnic table to eat our supper of cold cut sandwiches and chips. As we drank our bottles of water, we surveyed our campsite, which was void of life. I hoped to see a roadrunner, and perhaps a jack rabbit. Just when I thought I could relax after a full day of driving, "What are all those holes in the ground?"

"They're too small for prairie dogs, and there are too many to be snake holes," replied my husband.

"That's reassuring." I rubbed my hands together.

As the brilliant, reddish-orange sun set the sky on fire, ripples of red, yellow, brown, and purple coursed through the clay, mud, and sandstone, accented by veins of white gypsum. I recalled a quote by the artist Georgia O'Keeffe about Palo Duro Canyon. "It is a burning, seething cauldron, almost like a blast furnace full of dramatic light and color." What I initially perceived as a desolate, grim landscape became a mesmerizing tapestry of light and color.

As the evening temperatures cooled, fist-sized, brownish-black, fuzzy spiders emerged from quarter to half dollar sized holes. I didn't know they burrowed in the ground, and I'd never seen a live tarantula. They extended their bristly-haired legs with prominent black stripes as they scoured the hardened, clay terrain. "They're huge. They're everywhere." Hundreds blanketed the ground. "How will we get to our tent?" Images of a new horror movie, *Invasion of the Arachnids,* popped into my head. It did not have a happy ending. I slid closer to my husband and clutched his arm. "Sorry, but I've, I've never seen so many spiders. It makes my skin crawl." I clutched my knees. "Are they poisonous?"

"I'm sure their bite would get your attention, but I don't think their bite is life-threatening. Besides, they're more afraid of you. They'll move out of your way."

"I'm not so sure about that. I'm wearing open-toed sandals; you're not." I envisioned spiders climbing on my feet and my legs. I cringed.

However, the longer we watched them, the more fascinated I became. Their furry legs appeared to span several inches as they combed their territory methodically like game pieces being moved strategically on a chessboard. Apparently, they were hunting for their evening meal of grasshoppers, beetles, or small lizards. They waited patiently to pounce on unsuspecting prey. As it grew darker, I strained to see the multitude of spiders covering the ground like a bristly, polka dotted blanket. Eventually, the tarantulas began retreating back into their burrows. Feeling we could walk safely to our tent, we followed our flashlight beams and retreated to our tent for the evening. My husband zipped the tent flap closed.

As I approached my cot, I screamed, "What was that?"

"Where?" my husband asked.

"I saw something scoot under my cot." I gingerly picked up my feet. My husband cautiously scoured under my cot with his flashlight. "He's just a little, brown lizard. He looks a little like our fence lizards back home." Sometimes a fence lizard would sun himself on our front porch steps. "He's harmless."

"Well, get him out of here. I don't want company in my sleeping bag tonight." I implored. My husband's attempt to chase the prairie lizard out of our tent became quite comical as they ran in circles. The lightning-fast lizard eluded my husband's efforts. I dodged and then climbed onto my cot to get out of the way.

"Get the small tent broom and see if you can sweep him out when I chase him your way," directed my husband.

"Wait, I need to unzip the tent flap." I held the flap open with my trembling left hand and made a sweeping motion with my right hand. Apparently, the lizard had had enough exercise and excitement too, and he scurried out into the darkness. I tossed the broom down and quickly zipped the flap closed. We collapsed on our cots. I heard the eerie coyote howls echoing through the canyon. "Oh, no, how far is it to the bathroom?" I asked my husband.

The next morning we woke around 6:00 a.m. to the sharp, high dee-dee-dee of a killdeer; although upon leaving our tent, we never saw him. The orange and amber blaze of the sunrise over the rim of the gorge contrasted the cool morning air. We climbed from our tent and observed light and shadows shifting on colorful, banded layers of the canyon walls. Mist rose from the canyon floor. We caught a glimpse of a mountain bluebird as he flitted by our tent. We stood amazed at the masterful force of water that created Palo Duro Canyon, a treasure in the Panhandle of Texas.

Commanding Vistas

Rocky, snow-capped spires towered
over glacial-carved lake like sentinels
commanded by Mount Brown
protecting pristine water.

I strolled along the shore of
Lake McDonald in Glacier National Park.
The cool, Montana water lapped as gently
as rocking chairs on a front porch.

Clear water shimmered in the sunlight
like a pane of glass through which
I spotted colored pebbles of maroon,
jade, and lapis in the shallows.

I plunged my hand into the water and
retrieved an aquamarine stone.
I rubbed its smooth, chilled surface
with my fingertips. My muscles relaxed.

The fragrance of western red cedar
reminded me of the handmade cedar chest
my grandfather built that
sits at the foot of my bed.

The shrill of an elk pierced through still air.
My arm hair stood at attention
as the bugling echoed through the valley,
ascended to the snow-capped peaks.

Roaming Yellowstone

My husband and I were leery of tent camping in an unfamiliar wilderness with potential bear encounters, so we chose to stay in a rustic cabin in the Roosevelt/Tower area of Yellowstone National Park.

"Let's go on a horseback ride," suggested my husband, an experienced rider.

"Can't we just drive around?" A childhood memory of a horse rearing and throwing me off flashed through my mind. "It would be safer and faster." I rubbed the back of my neck.

"Hey, relax. They use trained horses on well-established trails." He patted my shoulder. "You'll be fine."

With reservation, I agreed to a two-hour horseback ride with an experienced guide at the Roosevelt Stables. I needed a boost to mount my chestnut quarter horse, Nutmeg, on this mild July morning. A dozen park visitors accompanied us on our trail ride. *Wonder if anyone else is as nervous as I am.* The horses assumed their positions in line. I was relieved that my husband would be right behind me. The well-schooled horses swished their tails to keep off flies and plodded along in single file along a well traversed, zig-zagging trail over uneven terrain. My horse stumbled over a tree root. I lurched forward, clutched the saddle horn, and gasped.

"Hold on," directed my husband.

I slid back in the western saddle as my horse climbed the hillside covered with juniper, white spruce, and Douglas fir. The air smelled of pine, leather, and salt. The trees were widely spaced, so I didn't have to duck branches. I could see beyond the horse's rump in front of me. Holding the reins, I grabbed the saddle horn, and scooted forward, but I slid back again despite my effort to press my thighs firmly into my horse's flanks.

Once we reached the crest of the hill, our horses fanned out along the ridgeline as if they had rehearsed for *Chorus Line.* The line-up provided all the riders with a panoramic view of Pleasant Valley. Bands of color formed waves like sports fans in a stadium. The flaming red and yellow Indian paintbrush and blue-violet camas and lupine struck me as more radiant than a Van Gogh painting. The spicy, bitter aroma of the silver, white, and black sage was overpowering at first. We saw hundreds of bison grazing on grasses and sedges in the meadows and sagebrush flats below. We listened to the bison grunts, snorts, and bellows carried on the wind. Their massive size and sheer numbers captivated me and carried me back in time.

I imagined a long-ago scene when millions of bison roamed the western prairies. I felt the ground tremble with their pounding hoofs as dust clouds rose. I smelled their musk. I heard the Arapaho songs and chants of their sun dance and summer solstice festival. I saw Arapaho warriors draped in bison hides armed with spears and bows and arrows readied for their seasonal hunt for these enormous beasts. Adrenalin surged, and beads of sweat formed on my forehead as I rode alongside these skilled, courageous hunters. I sensed the importance of the hunt to sustain the tribe over the harsh winter months. Then the high-pitched squeal of a bald eagle soaring overhead brought me back to the present.

Leaving the open plateau, we re-entered the woods along Lost Canyon and Lost Creek. I could understand how someone could get disoriented among the trees and uniform-colored rocks. *Wonder who named the canyon and creek "lost."* My stomach became queasy. The tree branches and canyon walls closed in on me. I redirected my attention to the canyon walls, and I scoured the rhyolite rock, hoping to see agile, big horn sheep navigate the narrow cliffs. I squinted, regretting that I had forgotten binoculars, to see moving grayish-brown specks on the steep canyon walls. In the distance, I heard the high shrill of bugling elk. The piercing sound, like fingernails scraping on a chalkboard, caused my arm hair to stand. The trail ascended over rocky, rolling terrain near Lost Creek Falls. I strained to hear the rushing water.

"Aren't we going to stop and see the waterfalls?" I hoped we would take a break and walk to the falls.

"No. The forty-foot falls are impressive in the spring when the mountain snows have melted, and the water volume is high. Now, very little water flows over the rocks. We're going on down to Lost Lake," stated our guide.

As we neared Lost Lake, the ground became marshy, and I worried that Nutmeg's hooves would get stuck in the mud. I hoped my horse would not sense my uneasiness. Convincing myself to rely on my horse's sure-footedness, Nutmeg maneuvered across a wooden plank walkway. Clickety-clack. Once across, I sighed and patted my horse's neck. "Good boy." The lake looked more like a large pond. Water lilies floated in the shallows, and white phlox, mauve prairie smoke, and silvery-purple sugar bowl clematis blooms created a floral mosaic along the shoreline. A small duck, resembling the coloration of a Canada goose, glided across the lake. Our guide informed us he was a male Barrow's goldeneye. Then I saw a white flash as a dark-eyed junco flew to a nearby juniper.

"Stay alert. We may see moose or black bear down by the lake," said our guide.

I had never seen a moose or a black bear in the wild. My muscles tensed. I was both excited and afraid of the possibility. *Would my horse bolt? Stay calm.*

"Don't worry. They'll hear us coming. They'll avoid us as long as we don't appear as a threat, especially to a mother and her young," assured our trail guide.

My heart raced, and my palms sweated. I was ready to advance. The path came out by what appeared to be a small cemetery, but what I thought were headstones were fossilized tree stumps.

"That's all that's left after people vandalized and took samples," explained our guide.

I shook my head. "It's a shame when people destroy public property."

"The park service placed a wrought-iron fence around the remaining, petrified, redwood tree to protect it."

Wonder how long it will remain intact. From there, our horseback ride wound through Pleasant Valley. The fragrance of the alpine meadow was intoxicating. I began humming, "The hills are alive, / With the sound of music, / With songs they have sung, / For a thousand years." I smelled a blend of vanilla, mint, lemon, and sweet corn. My mouth watered, and I longed for an ice cold, tart lemonade. To the south, I saw the barren, granite peak of Mount Washburn, towering over 10,000 feet. A fire tower sat atop the mountain like a candle on a cupcake.

"The views must be magnificent. How far can one see from the peak?" asked my husband.

"Depending on the weather and cloud cover, you can see as far as fifty miles. It's not unusual to see the snow-capped Teton Range."

Our guide pointed southeast. "Hiking Mount Washburn is beautiful this time of year with all the wildflowers in bloom." He smiled. "The hike is strenuous as you gain elevation."

"How far is the hike?" asked my husband.

"It's a six-mile round trip but plan to take at least half a day. A visitors' center and observation deck are on the lower levels of the fire tower. The views are incredible. If you have time, I highly recommend it."

"What do you think? Are you up for the hike?" my husband asked me.

"Perhaps, but not today. Let me get through this horseback ride first." I chuckled then grimaced. I was getting out of breath, and my legs ached just thinking about the hike. Again, I heard the high-pitched shrill of an elk. *It seems odd that an animal so large would make such a high-pitched sound.* Some members of the herd grazed while others lay near fallen trees. Several elk had impressive and intimidating antlers. I rubbed my neck thinking about the weight of their antlers and the impact of wolves and coyotes on the elk herds. We were up wind and far enough away that the elk did not seem troubled by our presence. Momentarily, I was immersed in nature and a time when mankind's imprint was not apparent. The soreness in my legs and back ended my liberation and caused me to push up my sleeve and glance at my watch. *Ten more minutes, I could make it.*

Our horses automatically sauntered back to the corral. Although my body longed for the trail ride to end, I desired to see more wildlife and breathtaking landscapes from a top my mount. In two hours, I had bonded with Nutmeg and was engaged wholly in my surroundings. After dismounting, I stroked my horse's neck. "Thank you for the ride of a lifetime."

Temporary Traces

Overnight anticipation,
I awaken to a
monochromatic canvas.
Fresh snow reveals
trails of crisscrossing
wildlife steps.
I behold deer hooves,
rabbit tracks, bird footprints.
Later more snowfall
erases my discoveries, creates
new monochromatic canvas,
for zig zagging patterns.

Wintry Treats

Morning flit, flutter
Frenzy at bird feeder
Chickadee alights on limb
Waiting its turn
Loose seeds sprinkle
Powdery snow below
Sparrows hop and peck
Exposing stirred up dirt
Doves sip through crack in ice
Thrushes feast on clusters
Of violet beautyberries
Persistent gray squirrel
Excavates black walnut
Clasps hidden treasure
Gnaws and chews

Once Millions Roamed

Prairie Drive winds through a spur of
Montana Mission Mountain Range.
A herd of 300 plus bison roam freely,
graze on Indian rice grass and basin wild rye.

Young bulls grunt, paw the ground,
and lower their heads.
Vehicle onlookers acknowledge
their territorial dominance
and hope for safe passage.

Traffic follows Mission Creek,
where bison drink and muddy waters.
They bound through brush.
Feet plod up an embankment.

Massive heads with matted fur emerge.
Pulses of visitors quicken, muscles tense.
Ground trembles as hoofs thunder
through the wildlife refuge
and raise clouds of tawny dust.

Thundering Hooves in the Land of Giants

I squirmed in my car seat and tapped my feet on the floorboard hurriedly as my husband and I drove into the National Bison Range in Montana. We opened our eyes wider. *Exhilaration or fear? Probably both.* I had only seen bison in a zoo, and only a few at that, so I was eager to gaze on a herd estimated at over 300 of the giants. We soon spied a cloud of ocher dust rising in the distance against the rugged peaks of the Mission Mountain Range.

As we approached the crest of a hill, two young bulls along the road grunted their disapproval at our territorial intrusion. They lowered their heads and pawed at the ground. My pulse quickened; my muscles tensed. These formidable beasts were unpredictable. Vulnerable, I sat in a rented Chevy Monza. In a charge, their massive, horned heads could crush our car like an aluminum can or easily flip it. My knuckles whitened as I gripped the edge of the car seat and prayed under my breath, "Please stay put. We are not a threat." We kept a close eye on the pair as my husband advanced the car slowly along Prairie Drive, a 14-mile loop following Mission Creek, where bison both drank and muddied the waters. We drove away from the agitated young bulls. I raised my face heavenward and whispered, "Thank you."

The creek along our route was bordered by a natural fence of thick buckthorn and coyote brush. Without warning, my husband stomped the brakes. I slammed forward, caught by my seat belt. I gasped. Enormous humps of dirty, matted brown fur plowed through the coyote brush like powerful locomotives. They bolted across the road into the meadow, wet mud coating their lower legs. The ground trembled beneath their thundering hooves. Their deep bellows resounded, reverberating in our vehicle. My adrenaline surged; my stomach became queasy.

"That was a close call," my husband declared, holding fast to the steering wheel. He raised his eyebrows and his voice. "I don't think they saw us."

"Either that or they're not intimidated by cars," I offered. "Do you think it's safe to drive on?" My heart pounded. I wrung my hands.

"We don't have much choice. This section of the road is one-way. I'll drive slowly, stay alert." His voice was reassuring. He eased his foot off the brake. The speedometer inched up to 25 mph.

We scanned both sides of the road, listening intently for any warning signals—a snort or a grunt. What was going to be an intriguing adventure among free-roaming bison in the Montana countryside was a nerve-wracking game of hide-and-seek. Although close encounters with the bison excited me, the thought of a one-ton animal ramming into the side of the car terrified me.

Our Chevy crept up the ascending roadway. Reaching a plateau, we pulled into a scenic overlook. Still fearful of a stray monstrous creature charging at 35 mph, we chose not to get out of the car. Instead, we opened our car windows for a better look. We enjoyed the spiced-honey aroma of blue elderberries and the piney, citrusy scent of the Monterey pines, especially preferred over the musky odor of bison. Now at a safe distance, I appreciated the opportunity to observe these magnificent creatures. At least 50 bison grazed on rye grass and wild oats in the valley below. The cows and their calves moved along, grazing methodically. I thought about a time when millions of bison populated the western prairies and waves of brown, shaggy beasts foraged on meadows of barley and wild rye. They must have been a compelling sight. I recalled reading how valuable bison were to Native Americans for meat and hides. A pair of frisky calves shook their heads and galloped as if playing a game of tag. My husband and I chuckled at their antics. The cows tried to corral the youngsters, reminding me of teachers gathering their students at the end of recess. A few mule deer grazed on the fringe of the bison herd; we could hear a bald eagle squawk overhead. I envisioned a startled herd stampeding, trampling everything in their path. I imagined the deafening sound of pounding hooves, clouds of choking dust, flying clumps of grass, and massive silhouettes casting long shadows across the plains.

As we pulled back onto the road to drive the last segment of the loop, what would keep this herd of 300 from being startled by a passing car of curious visitors? The massive size and power of the bison commanded my respect, but I was not relieved until our tiny car passed unscathed through the final gate of the National Bison Range beyond the world of these giants.

River Gifts

In my daredevil youth, on steamy summer afternoons,
seeking the thrill of rafting down a rushing river,
jostled by the rapids,
dodging logs,
ricocheting off rocks,
bobbing up and down like a cork,
listening to the water grumble,
beseeching me, "Slow down."
Intensely focusing on my course,
scraping past more nested boulders,
taking risks, and overcoming challenges.
Exhilarating feats despite the cost—
If only I had sought an eddy
for respite and reflection.

Now in my advanced years,
preferring more tranquil rides,
tube floating down a calm river,
spying my reflection in the glassy surface,
dangling my feet and hands in the refreshing water,
drifting down the placid channel,
cradled by the gentle current,
welcoming the river's gurgles,
"Take it easy; enjoy the scenery."

Appreciating the shallow, amber water
transitioning to deep, bottle green at mid-stream,
sunlight shimmering off the riverbed's sediment,
fish gently tickling my toes,
a wood duck paddling gracefully,
turtles sunning on a fallen tree trunk,
birds cheerfully serenading,
and honeysuckle's sweet, floral fragrance
wafting in the breeze.

A predictable course with no unforeseen obstacles,
just cruising through life,
confident that I'm prepared
for whatever lies ahead.

Having traveled down this meandering river many times,
I now bid the river a final good-bye.
Soon, too, will I be retiring,
peaceful and content.

Outside My Window

What lies outside my window?

Ruby-throated hummingbirds
    dart, hover, and perform
    entertaining acrobatics

Red-spotted purple admiral butterfly
    alights upon blush cosmos,
    sips warmed nectar

House sparrow perches on stones
    in a wrought-iron birdbath
    then quenches her thirst

Two potted chrysanthemums display
    red-tipped yellow petals and
    dark lavender blooms

Brass wind chimes dangle
    from shepherd's hook,
    ding in the summer breeze

Musical melody
    complements
    prismatic colors

What lies outside my window?
    pleasant views that
    enliven my spirit

About the Author

Suzanne Cottrell is the author of three poetry chapbooks: *Gifts of the Seasons, Autumn and Winter; Gifts of the Seasons, Spring and Summer;* and *Scarred Resilience* (Kelsay Books). Her poems have appeared in numerous anthologies and journals, including the *Avocet, Plum Tree Tavern, Poetry Quarterly, The Pangolin Review, Burningword Literary Journal,* and *Vita Press Anthologies* while her prose has appeared in journals and anthologies, including *The Dead Mule School of Southern Literature, Flash Fiction Magazine, Dragon Poet Review, Nailpolish Stories, Dual Coast Magazine, Quail Bell Magazine,* Personal Story Publishing Project anthologies, Inwood Indiana Press anthologies, and Quillkeepers Press anthologies. Suzanne is an outdoor enthusiast and retired teacher, who enjoys reading, writing, knitting, hiking, Pilates and yoga. Read more about her writing journey at www.suzanneswords.com.

www.ingramcontent.com/pod-product-compliance
Lightning Source LLC
Chambersburg PA
CBHW022140160426
43197CB00009B/1370